19882

Handmade Rugs
from practically anything

by Jean Ray Laury and Joyce Aiken

Photographs by Gayle Smalley

Distributed to the trade by
Doubleday & Company, Inc.
Garden City, New York

COUNTRYSIDE PRESS
a division of Farm Journal, Inc.
Philadelphia

Copyright © 1971, 1972 by Jean Ray Laury and Joyce Aiken
Published by Countryside Press
  a division of Farm Journal, Inc.
Distributed to the trade by
  Doubleday & Company, Inc.
  Garden City, New York
All rights reserved
Printed in the United States of America

All rugs pictured in this book are the work of
the authors or of other designers as indicated
All drawings and illustrations: the authors

Book design: Hal Lose, Al J. Reagan
Photography: Gayle Smalley—except
    Number 79 Carolyn Heddins,
    80 Dr. Foster Marlow
    Color: Number 6 Randy Miller,
    3, 8 Richard Gross

Library of Congress Catalog Card Number 70-185588

19882

Introduction

Rug making is not just fun, it is a useful pastime for anyone who wants to be creatively busy while relaxing, visiting or watching television. In this book are rug ideas you are not likely to find at your state fair or at regional crafts exhibits. Though made from ordinary materials, the rugs are distinctive and exciting.

The authors, Jean Ray Laury and Joyce Aiken, are free-lance designers. They have more than 10 years experience teaching rug making and other handcrafts to children, college students and adults. They know well the pitfalls for amateur rug makers, and have developed techniques which make rug making easy for anyone who can follow simple instructions. More than 150 illustrations, many in color, offer proof of their own special talents for using humble materials in surprising ways and for motivating others to do likewise. Some of the photographed work was completed by their students, some by friends who are also professional craftsmen.

We got the idea for this book when we saw the exciting work the students were doing and we realized why: Mrs. Laury and Mrs. Aiken don't teach rug making—they *inspire* rug making! We wish we could lay the rugs themselves at your feet. Short of that, we offer this book with the conviction that you will catch their enthusiasm for creating rugs . . . and achieve the ultimate joy of seeing your own creations in use.

Rachel Martens
Crafts / Home Furnishings Editor
FARM JOURNAL

Contents

1. "White Landscape"   3x6'   by Darlene Huckobey.
A rich sculptural surface results from the use of
long and short yarns in this white-on-white rug.

Handmade Rugs

Of all the home crafts, rug making is certainly among the most humble. Those of us who make rugs are not usually aspiring to a gallery show. If a rug is of an exceptional nature, then of course it may be displayed. But the real function of the rug, and the purpose for making it, have to do with the home.

Specific purposes may vary . . . you may wish to have a rug that a three-year-old can wiggle her toes in as she gets out of bed in the morning. Or you may want a brilliant splash of red or orange near a window seat. Or you may even just want to catch a major portion of the dripping water from your back-yard swimmers. But whichever of these it might be, the rug goes on the floor and it is going to be stepped on. It will function, or work, and fulfill its purpose in that sense. What further attributes it has in the way of texture or pattern or color are aspects of rug making that keep it intriguing, exciting, and timeless.

The rug offers every homemaker an opportunity to bring some of her own creative energies and ideas into the practical functioning of her home. Almost every home has a closet (or a drawer, or a box) which contains the essentials for making a rug—leftover yarns, faded blue jeans, used clothes or old curtains. Much of the joy and challenge in rug making comes from the use of these old materials, scraps, and leftovers. The whole idea of making something from almost nothing makes a game of it. A few generations back, salvage was an essential aspect of making rugs, since materials were hard to come by, and feet

had to be kept from the cold of the floors. Now we may use the same materials and approaches not so much of necessity as desire, along with an awareness of the absurdity of waste and the luxury of hand-crafted work. Besides the use of scrap materials, we have available today a wide range of fabrics, colors and textures. Many are inexpensive, some are treated to resist soiling, and all can be found in almost any department store or fabric shop.

There is more to the rug, of course, than the finished usable product. The making of the rug involves design decisions in color, form, method and technique. It is a field of wide range—open to the child who can thread one strip of cloth through another, as well as to the experienced craftsman. Rug making has unlimited possibilities for the designer, or for the homemaker who has not yet really exercised her creative skills.

The available range in rugs is diverse since our needs and uses for them vary so much. A rug that is suitable at the foot of Grandmother's rocker may not be suitable by the back door. Some rugs may be selected, before they ever get to the floor, for use as chair or bench pads, as wall hangings, on counters for potted plants, or as car or lap robes. The weight, backing, and the material all combine in appropriate combinations for certain uses.

Anyone who wishes to, can make a rug. It is our purpose in this book to help that person. The different ways of working which are shown will help each person find those methods which seem most appropriate, most easily managed or most readily available.

There are rugs in this book which can be made by children, and many which require no special tools, skills or equipment. We have avoided the use of rugs which require complex looms or special equipment. The only tools used are very simple, and the looms are those which can be made at home. Your own time and energy for these projects will grow as your work develops and designs take form.

Before starting, it may help to ask yourself some questions. Is there a method you particularly want to try? Are there colors you especially want to use? Is there a specific place the rug is to be used? Do you have a certain person in mind? If you have a basket full of old wool clothes, and need a good sturdy rug near the back door, you may wish to do a braided rug. If you have a favorite reading chair where you like to curl up with a book but the area needs some color, perhaps a button rug might well be your first project. If your children (or the Brownie troop) want to work, they could enjoy doing a hoop or button rug. Answer as many questions as you can about how, where and for whom. Then take a look at what is available (at home or to purchase) and start from there.

You may wish to make a rug just because you are inspired by one in a photograph, or because you find materials in a favorite color. Go ahead and make the rug in the colors you like and there will be a spot in your home where it can be used. If it really doesn't fit, you have a Christmas present on hand.

There are few homes which cannot use another area rug. But even if you give the rug away, the pleasure of making it remains yours.

2. ''Green Grow the Flowers Oh''   3′ diameter
by Jean Ray Laury. Machine-appliqué satin stitch outlines each
of the cut felt pieces in this ball-fringed circle.

1

MACHINE APPLIQUÉ RUGS

If you are longing to add a brilliant splash of blue or magenta to a room and you want to accomplish it with great speed, then machine-appliqué felt is for you! Felt is more durable than you might guess and, used in layers or overlapped, it becomes even stronger.

Using a sewing machine makes the work speedy and neat. Stitching may be accomplished with a straight stitch or a satin stitch and examples of each are shown.

About Felt. In purchasing your felt material look for felts which are 50% wool (or more). Most available felts are half wool and half rayon, but check. One that is 75% rayon will not wear as well as those with more wool fiber. Felts also come in different gauges or thicknesses, though you rarely have a choice of gauge in those available to you. It may help to hold the felt up to the light . . . if you can see through it or if the fibers seem unevenly distributed, it may not wear well. Most fabric shops or department stores stock a half-wool felt, or can give you information about the fiber content of their stock.

If you wish to use an *all*-wool felt, or cannot locate the 50% wool felt in a fabric shop, your best source will be to order through an interior decorator. Most decorator shops have the color charts showing an entire range of colors and will order the color you choose. The usual minimum cut is one yard, and if you use an all-wool background it is then satisfactory to use a part-wool felt for the appliqué.

A finished felt rug lies flat and looks best used as an area rug over carpeting. If you plan to use the rug on a wood, tile, linoleum or other smooth or polished surface, be sure to use a rubber rug pad beneath the felt to prevent skidding or slipping. Felts are not washable and must be dry-cleaned, though the wool fibers resist soiling to some extent. Polyester felts may soon be on the market and they would, of course, be washable.

Making The Rug. Felt colors are brilliant and flat and lend themselves beautifully to appliqué. The simple straight stitch was used in "Forest", Plate 3. First, a circle was cut from the forest green felt. To cut the circle a pattern may first be made on paper following this procedure: Tie a thread to a large pin (or a nail or tack). Then tie a pencil to the other end of the thread. Insert the pin in the center of the sheet of paper so that it stands vertically or hold it there if necessary. Pull the thread taut (making it longer or shorter as needed) and trace a circle with your pencil. See Drawing 4 which shows how this is accomplished.

Once the paper circle is cut accurately, it can be pinned to the felt. Mark the circumference with a chalk line or you can cut the circle from the pattern. If you plan to use a fringe or an edging on the finished rug, unevenness in the circle will not matter. If the

3. "Forest"   3' diameter   by Jean Ray Laury. Pie-shaped
wedges of white provide a shape from which the trees are cut.

cut edge is the finished edge, you will want to cut with care to keep the line smooth.

To work out an all-over pattern, as in "Forest", use your circular paper pattern to draw on. By taking the paper circle and dividing it into sections, you can determine the area to be filled by one plant or tree. See Drawing 5. This way, you know that all the forms will fit back into the circle.

Next, cut the shapes in felt. Since felt is a nonwoven material, there is no grain or direction and the appliqué pieces may be placed in any way on the material.

When the appliqué shapes have been cut, pin them in place on the felt background. Machine-stitch, using a fairly long stitch. Set the stitch length at 8 to 10 for most machines. The stitches should be closer than a basting stitch, but not as tight as one used in sewing clothing. The line of stitches should be about ⅛ inch from the edge. See detail of the stitching in Plate 6. If you pin carefully, it is not necessary to machine-baste. If you have any difficulty with the sewing, do a hand-basted stitch about ½ inch from the edge. Then machine-sew between the cut edge and the basting stitch. Drawing 7 shows the proper placement.

"Forest" was edged with a cotton ball fringe, sewn under the outer edge of the rug. In this one the band does not show and only the row of cotton balls appears at the edge. "Forest" uses a white thread on the appliqué of the white felt which tends to hide the stitching. However, a color could also be used for additional contrast and pattern so that the stitched line could become a stronger element in the design.

"Soft Garden" is also sewn with a straight machine-stitch. The felt, however, is torn or pulled rather than cut. This gives a soft blurred edge in contrast to the sharp-cut

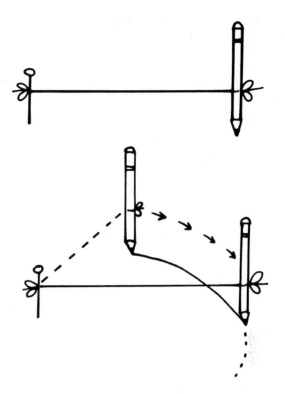

4. A simple compass made with a pin, thread and pencil is used to draw a large circle pattern for a round rug. Length of thread is the radius of circle.

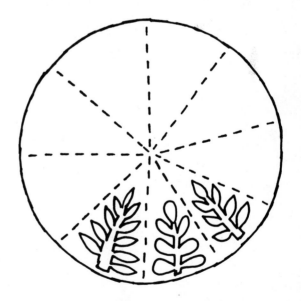

5. Sections of the circle indicate the area into which each design unit shall fit.

6. "Forest" detail—straight machine
stitching outlines each of the cut shapes.

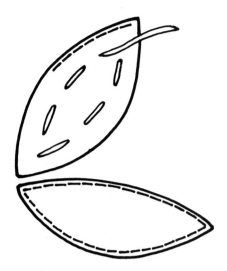

7. Large basting stitches hold the felt shapes in place, machine stitches are close to the cut edge.

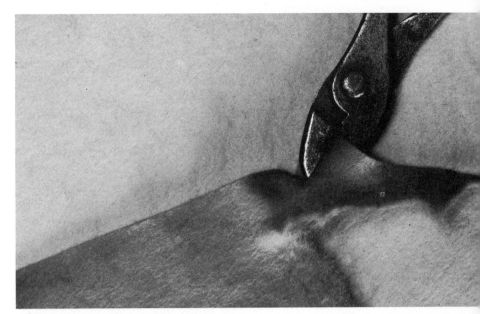

8. Pulled felt detail—pliers are used to pull the felt, leaving a soft frayed edge.

9. "Soft Garden" detail—the pulled or torn edge gives the flowers a blurred look.

edge. Plate 8 shows how this is done. Tearing or pulling the felt is not easy, but the effect makes it worth the extra effort. A thinner "cheaper" felt will tear more easily. Some half-wool felts are cross-carded, making tearing more difficult though not impossible. If thinner felt is used for tearing, the background should still be wool or half-wool. "Soft Garden" was torn, with pliers, from half-wool felt.

Plate 9 shows some of the torn shapes, pinned into place. A detail of the stitching appears in Plate 10, followed by a picture of the whole rug in Plate 11.

It may seem easier to cut shapes first as desired and to then pull or fray the edges by using pliers. The soft torn edge can be used effectively in combination with the clear, sharp-cut edges.

The zigzag stitch gives a smooth outline to the appliquéd felt. The zigzag is used closed, or tight, in what is called the satin stitch. This stitching does require that shapes be machine-basted first. The basting stitch is also a zigzag, open and narrower than the finished satin stitch. Drawing 14 shows the steps of the machine satin stitching.

Plate 15 shows a detail of "Green Grow the Flowers Oh". The shapes are simple, making the sewing easy. In the overall view of it, Plate 2, the simple stem forms which are sewn first radiate from the center. Then leaves and flowers are placed in relationship to the stems.

The satin stitching gives a smooth line edge to the felt and holds the appliqué very securely in place. These machine-appliqué felts are durable and will withstand fairly heavy use. For the appliqué stitch, use a thread color that blends with the felt color

10. "Soft Garden" detail—after the pulled felt shapes are pinned, a line of straight stitching secures them in place.

11. ''Soft Garden''   42″ square   by Jean Ray Laury.
Sharp lines of machine stitching contrast to the soft edges
of pulled felt in this rug of pale greens and blues.

12. "Pedestal"   36x40"   by Jean Ray Laury. Colored strips of felt
are folded and cut into decorative shapes to provide a simple rug design.

without exactly matching. For example, where the flowers are in orange, pink and red, it may add a more decorative edge to use pink thread on the red felt, red on the orange felt, and orange on the pink felt instead of matching color to color. See Color Plate 9 for another look at this floral rug. The edging on this rug is a cotton ball fringe, used this time with the fringe on *top* of the white felt, which gives a band of red along with the red balls.

"Pedestals" in Plate 12, also machine appliqué, uses strips of felt for the basic design. The approach to design here is very simple and the strips need not be cut into more elaborate pedestal forms. A background is first selected and cut to size. Then bands of felt, cut from related or contrasting colors, are placed over the background, going from one edge across to the other. See Color Plate 2. These bands of felt can be left simple and plain or they may be more elaborately decorated. Drawing 16 suggests other rugs using bands as the basic element of design.

The primary advantage to using bands is that they facilitate efficient use of material. When a cut is made, both the cut shape and the "leftover" shape (or negative shape) are usable. A single cut provides the beginnings of two shapes. See Drawing 13.

Inexpensive fringes may be found in stores that sell awnings, canvas, and curtain edgings; and in many department stores and fabric shops. If you buy an off-white or natural fringe it can easily be dyed at home; but be sure to include ample fringe to allow for shrinking.

Machine appliqué provides a fast, easy and effective means for producing a handmade rug. There are limitless possibilities with this method and it is easily and often combined with other methods. The sewing machine is an essential tool to some of the rugs shown in the chapters on Cut-Through Rugs and Strip Rugs. *19882*

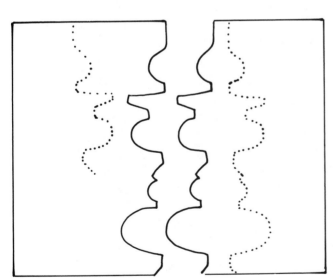

13. Both positive and negative shapes are usable so that when one cut is made, two shapes occur.

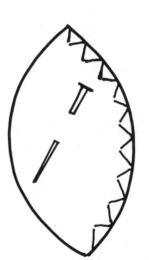

14. After the cut piece is pinned in place a narrow but open zigzag stitch bastes it in place. A wide satin stitch then covers the basting.

15. "Green Grow the Flowers Oh" detail—machine
satin stitches give a smooth outline to the cut felt shape

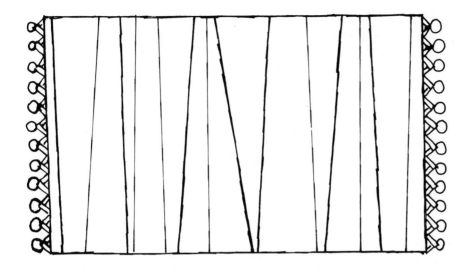

16. Using bands as a basic
pattern, many design
variations are possible.

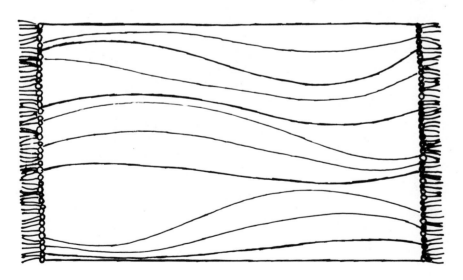

17. "Stars and Stripes" 40x58" by Joyce Aiken.
The straight or running stitch is used to apply the squares,
rectangles and stars in this hand-appliqué rug.

2

HAND APPLIQUÉ RUGS

Hand-sewn felt appliqué rugs provide opportunity for the stitcher to use her skills. The stitches themselves add textural interest to the edges of the appliqué pieces as they pucker slightly or draw in as the thread is pulled tight. If you have no sewing machine, or if you prefer to work at a table or on your lap, then hand sewing is for you. The primary advantage of hand sewing is its portability.

A good firm running stitch is fairly strong; you need not be too concerned that it will come apart. Of course, if a thread does break, it is easily sewn again. The running stitch (or simple stitch or straight stitch) is easy, fast and effective. It is a stitch which a child can manage without difficulty. If you prefer an edge that is sewn more firmly, the overcast stitch or the buttonhole stitch (shown in the chapter on Button Rugs) may be better.

"Stars and Stripes" in Plate 17 and Color Plate 15 is a brilliant arrangement of red, white and blue. The big blocks, cut 9 inches square, offer a checker board effect. This gives the rug a total design and within this pattern of blocks variations on stars and stripes are seen. Some fabric shops carry precut 9-inch squares. The blocks are sewn first to the background piece of felt. A running stitch uses heavy duty mercerized thread about ⅛ inch from the cut edge of the felt. In sewing squares, start at one corner and have the block pinned in place. Do

not use so many pins that sewing is made difficult . . . just five or six will do.

To give a finer look to your stitching, do a running stitch which conceals the longest half of the stitch on the underneath side of the fabric. The part of the stitch that shows is small, making the stitches look delicate and fine. Drawing 18 shows how this is accomplished. If you would feel safer sewing with a double thread, use two threads through one needle rather than knotting the two ends of a single thread. See Drawing 19. This will keep your thread from twisting and making some stitches look less smooth and uneven.

The "Alphabet" rug is also a hand-sewn piece. While this one is used as a wall hanging, the method is the same as that used for a rug. Again an overall pattern of squares covers the entire panel. These blocks are 4 inches square and Plate 20 shows them attached to a backing panel. A running stitch was used to appliqué all pieces. Plate 21 shows some of the cut pieces pinned in place. It is not necessary to baste, but use only a few pins. The next photograph, Plate 22, shows the same area after it is stitched. Hand-sewn details appear in Plate 23. Finally, the finished panel is seen in Plate 24. Any combination of letters, numbers, objects, toys or people could be adapted to such a rug for a child. If you feel uncertain about your own lettering, use ads from newspapers or magazines to help you. An assortment of

20. ''Alphabet'' detail—blocks, cut 4″ square, are sewn to the backing with a running stitch using a single strand of embroidery floss.

21. Cutouts are added to the blocks and spaces and then are pinned in place.

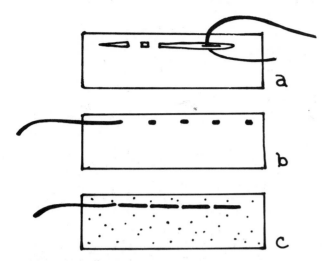

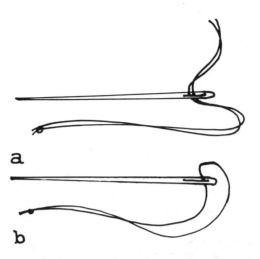

18. Running stitches are made with the small part of the thread showing on the surface, as in a. and b. The reverse side of the material is shown in c.

19. To use double thread for sewing, put two threads through the needle as in a. If one thread is used and doubled, as in b., the threads may twist and the sewn line will not be as smooth.

22. As cutouts are sewn, others are pinned in place.

23. When appliqué is finished, some embroidery stitches and French knots are used for decorative effect.

26

24. "Alphabet" 34x42" by Jean Ray Laury.
The completed rug is finished with a fringe, dyed blue to complement
the blues, greens and limes of the backing and blocks.

different styles of letters and numbers will also add to the design. However, if you are doing a panel expressly to help a child learn letters rather than to provide a decorative and colorful hanging, it might be better to use block letters which are more easily recognized by the learning reader. Drawings 25 and 27 suggest other ideas especially adaptable for hand-sewn rugs.

While blocks or squares provide a good overall basic pattern, making the decorative aspect of the work much simpler, hand-sewn appliqué is not limited to this. Plate 26, "Yellow Weed", depicts a felt appliqué on heavy twill backing. The running stitch is pulled tight, so that edges are held firmly in place. Any backing fabric that seems too light weight can be thickened by the addition of extra layers either of the same fabric or a different one. For example, if a light canvas was used and the rug did not have enough body, a piece of burlap, another layer of canvas, a layer of felt or upholstery material could be used. It should be sewn at the outside edges and then tacked several places in the center, or rubber rug padding (available in stores which sell floor coverings) can be tacked to the back. Rubber padding for runners usually comes 24 inches or 36 inches wide, and can be purchased by the foot. It will be sufficient for most rugs.

Hand stitching can be effectively combined with machine appliqué as seen in the rug detail of Plate 28 of the "Golden Sunflower".

Hand sewing appears in some of the other chapters as well . . . namely, the Cut-Through and Button Rugs. With a minimum of tools and equipment, the hand-sewn rug makes possible a whole range of rug making ideas.

25. A simple circular form suggests the sun in an easily sewn hand-appliqué rug.

26. "Yellow Weeds" detail—running stitches, pulled tight, tend to draw the edges of the felt into a slight pucker, adding more interest to the otherwise flat felt.

27. Another variation of the circle results in a more elaborate sun. Where colors change, one felt piece may be stacked on top of another.

28. "Golden Sunflower" detail—the smooth edge of machine appliqué contrasts to the hand stitching of the circles.

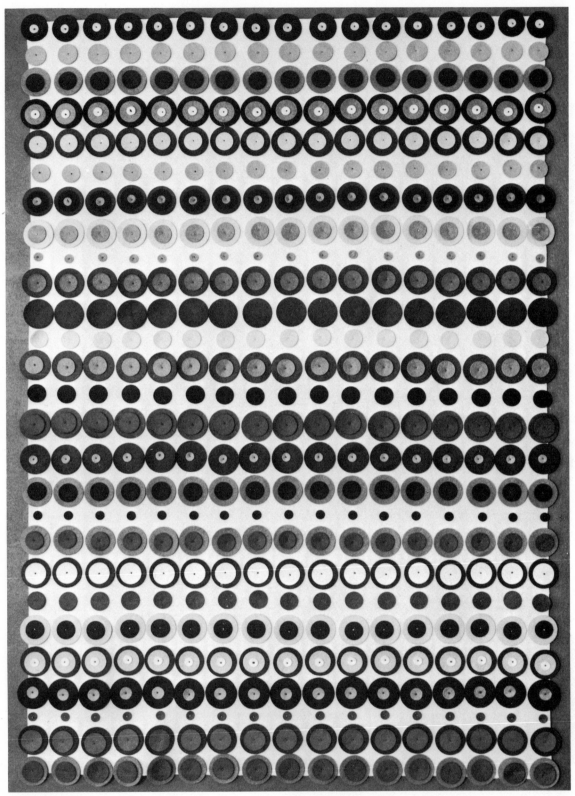

29. "Dot - Dit - Dot" 36x42" by Jean Ray Laury. Bright
colored circles of felt are stacked to make this "pop" panel rug.

3

BUTTON RUGS

The traditional old-fashioned button rug was one which used several felt circles stacked on a wool background—all of which were held together by sewing through the layers to attach a button on top. The buttons seem uninviting on soft felts, so they have been eliminated in those shown here. Several contemporary adaptations of that basic rug method are covered in this chapter.

"Dot-Dit-Dot" in Plate 29 shows circles used singly or in stacks of two or three. The rectangular base fabric (felt or heavy wool fabric work fine) is cut first and colors are selected to contrast with that background. Here the circles are added in rows, placing one row at a time. A French knot is used to attach each stack so that the knot appears on top. These knots are sewn using three strands of embroidery floss; each knot is securely tied on the back side. Plate 30 shows a detail of the knots.

After cutting 20 to 30 circles—using various-sized objects (glasses, salt shakers, spice bottles, etc.) for patterns—you, too, will start looking for an easier way. Most gasket companies have ready-made dies used for punching circles from various industrial materials. They use a pneumatic press, placing the circle die over 8 to 10 layers of felt at a time. It operates a little like a large paper punch with no handle. If you pursue this possibility in your own city, be sure to ask the gasket company if they have the dies. Charges for this work are based on an hourly fee for the use of the machine and operator (no, they will not let you operate it yourself!) so have your felt colors stacked and ready before taking them to the shop. In our experience, about 15 minutes worth of die-cutting and you can make button rugs for a month!

If you use large circles, say an inch or more in diameter, you may find that a single French knot doesn't adequately hold the material in place. You may add more knots, or you can sew the outside of the circle with either of two simple stitches.

Plate 31 shows a detail of the overcast stitch used to firmly attach circles to the base fabric. A heavy duty thread may be used, or a strand of embroidery floss. If you wish the stitches to show add a detail and pattern to the edge, use thread of contrasting color. A matching thread will, of course, conceal the stitches.

The buttonhole stitch or blanket stitch is shown in Plate 32. In this one, as well as the overcast stitch, the largest circle or outside

30. "The Squares" detail—French knot at the center holds a stack of felt circles in place. More knots may be added to make the surface tighter if it is to be used as a rug.

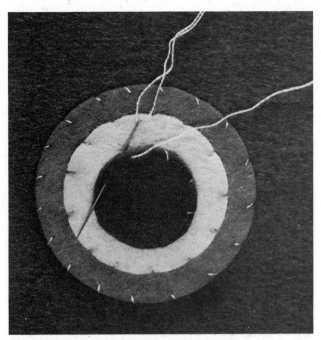

31. Overcast stitch detail—the easy-to-do overcast stitch holds circles firmly for a rug.

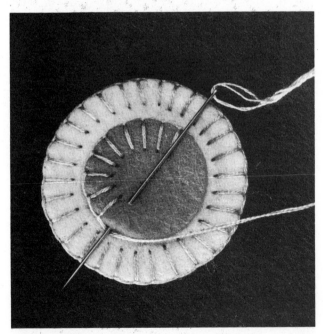

32. Buttonhole stitch detail—Buttonhole stitches make a durable edge on appliqué felt.

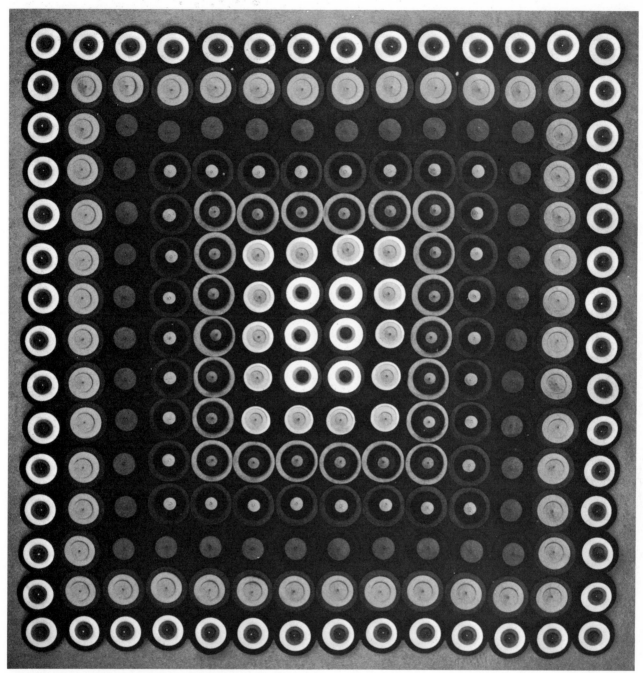

33. "The Squares" 34x34" by Jean Ray Laury.
Die-cut circles are stacked and knotted
in place in this bright colored variation
of the old-fashioned button rug.

one should be sewn in place first. This makes the smaller circles easier to handle. Either of these stitches will make your button rug firmer, and less susceptible to wear.

Geometric use of the stacked circles or buttons on a base fabric is shown in Plate 33. For this geometric design, place the circles an inch or 2 from the edge of the base fabric. When all the circles have been placed and stitched, the backing can be cut away all around so that a scalloped edge results. This rug is also shown in Color Plate 5.

"Crimson Bouquet", Color Plate 4, is another variation of the button rug. Here circles of all sizes were cut freehand. Then the circles were varied by scalloping them or cutting them into petal shapes. These are stacked four, five or six layers thick, and French knots sometimes are added at petal ends to help hold flowers in place. See Drawing 34. Plate 37 shows the entire rug.

Flowers in "Crimson Bouquet" are placed in a random all-over arrangement. To assist in cutting scallops or petals evenly, try dividing the circle into sections first. Clip in from each side, dividing the circle first in halves, then fourths, then eighths. Drawing 35 shows how this is done. After making the clips (each of the same depth), round off each corner as shown. For a six-petal flower, start out the same by dividing the circle in halves. Then cut each half into three portions. The notched flowers are even simpler. Just clip as for petals and then notch at each clipping. See Drawing 36.

"The Button Rug" concept may be an old one, but certainly its application is contemporary. The method is not limited to rugs. Stitchery panels and wall hangings can make use of this same approach.

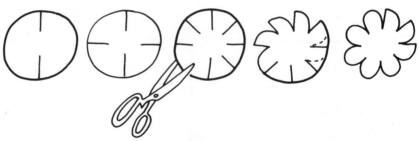

34. French knots which hold flowers in place also add a decorative detail to the rug.

35. To simplify the cutting of flower shapes, first cut out a circle. Clip in from the edge to divide the circle into eight portions, then round off each portion.

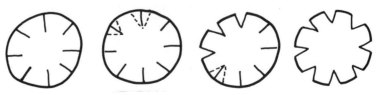

36. Notched flowers are also cut from circles. Clip, as indicated, then notch the fabric at each clip.

37. "Crimson Bouquet" 30x36" by Jean Ray Laury.
Flowers of all shapes and sizes, cut free-hand, are combined
with circles in this brightly patterned rug.

38. "Mrs. McKenzie's Garden" 36x54" by Jean Ray Laury.
Layers of felt are stacked three or four deep in this cut-through
rug. Additional colors may then be used in the appliqué.

4

CUT-THROUGH RUGS

Cut-through rugs make use of a stitchery technique called either cut-through work or reverse appliqué. In this approach, several layers (2, 3 or 4) of felt are cut to the desired rug size and stacked one on top of another. They are then pinned or basted to hold the edges securely together. Cutting is started through the top layer, revealing the second. Cutting through this layer reveals the third.

A circular shape suggesting the sun, makes a good simple form with which to begin. Plate 39 shows the three layers stacked and pinned with the first circle cut out. In the next step, Plate 40, a second circle has been cut to reveal the bottom layer. With more cutting completed, the three-color pattern begins to develop, Plate 41.

"Mrs. McKenzie's Garden" in Plate 38 is a cut-through rug, and a detail appears in Plate 42. This one is hand-sewn and uses a stack with orange on top, then red with ma-genta as a base. For cutting this complex three-stack, it is necessary to pin the cut shapes or baste them as you progress. This rug appears in Color Plate 1.

A detail of "Yellow Windows" is seen in Plate 43. Here, a gold was placed on top of yellow and machine-stitched lines were crisscrossed over the rug. See Drawing 44. Machine stitching produces a series of rectangles. Smaller rectangles are then cut out inside each one. These vary in size and each cut rectangle is removed. See Drawing 45. After all rectangles are cut out, a variety of yellow and gold felts are used as inserts—slipped inside the rectangular opening. These rectangular inserts are cut slightly smaller than the crisscross stitched areas, so they will slip inside to fit and lie flat. Then machine stitching is used on the inside, or smaller rectangle, to hold the inserts in place. The rug is edged with ball fringe.

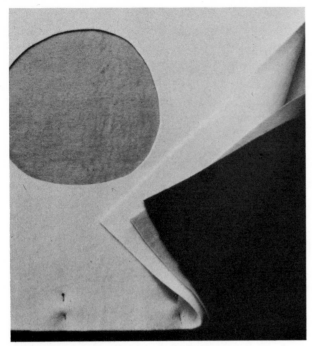

39. Cut-through detail—felts are stacked and pinned or basted before the first cut is made.

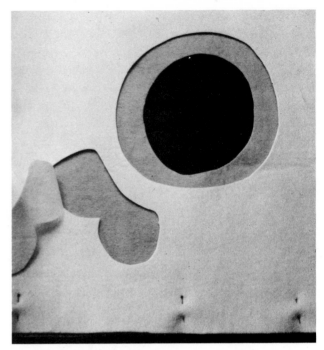

40. Inside the first circle, a second circle is cut, revealing the layer beneath it.

41. As shapes are repeated in the three colors, the design begins to take on some complexity.

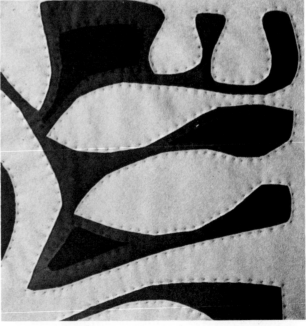

42. "Mrs. McKenzie's Garden" detail—cut edges are sewn with a running stitch or, if they are pinned and basted, a machine stitch can be used.

"Yellow Windows" is used as a counter cover in Plate 46.

"Low Tide" is an example of a two-color cut-through. See Plate 47. Here, a gold felt was placed over yellow and then the swirling lines were sewn with a straight stitch on the sewing machine. After the sewing was completed, areas of the felt were cut and removed. Narrow gold fringe was then inserted under the edges of the cut felt, as seen in the detail of Plate 48.

Because the cut-through technique provides for layering of felts, the finished rugs have good weight and body which helps them to lie flat and remain in place. The possibilities in working cut-through suggest the full range: hand or machine sewing, natural forms or geometric—as simple or as complex as the rug maker wishes. Cut-through rugs are worthy of being hung on the wall, or the technique may be used for pillows.

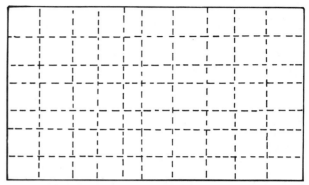

44. Machine-stitched lines of varying widths divide this rug top into a pattern of squares and rectangles.

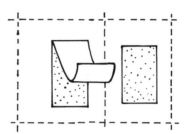

45. Rectangles are cut and removed from within the stitched areas.

43. "Yellow Windows" detail—two layers of felt were stacked in this cut-through, and a grid-pattern was machine-stitched through them both.

46. "Yellow Windows" 24x36"
by Joyce Aiken. Assorted yellow
and gold inserts (left) make the
window colors vary from light to dark
and from pale to brilliant.

47. "Low Tide" 3x5' by
Joyce Aiken. Yellow and gold
felts are combined with fringes
in this machine-stitched rug.

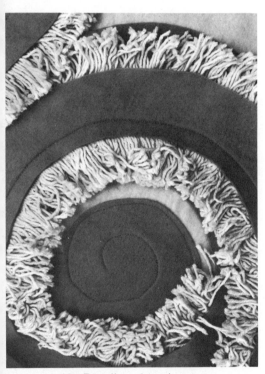

48. Detail—after the cut
areas were removed, fringes
were inserted and sewn in
place, again using a straight
machine stitch.

49. Macramé Rug   7′ diameter   by Sue Donleavey.
Using only square knots, this lace-like macramé rug repeats
a circular pattern in quarter-inch nylon rope.

5

MACRAMÉ AND ROPE RUGS

Macramé, the art of tying knots, has been practiced for centuries by sailors and was recently revived into an enormously popular craft. There are numerous good books available now with instructions for doing macramé. Many magazines recently have also carried articles and instructions. For those of you who have found this an intriguing craft, rug making will offer you an opportunity to use your macramé knotting in new ways and on large-scale projects.

Plate 49 shows a 7-foot round macramé rug made with 1500 feet of ¼-inch nylon rope. The rug was started in the center and worked entirely with square knots. As the rug grew larger, more rope was added until a heavy band of square knot sinnets finished the edge. Scattered overhand knots were used at the ends of the ropes for fringe.

It is important that you use the right kind of cord or rope for doing macramé. Nylon rope is a good choice because it clearly shows the knot pattern as seen in Plate 50. A rope with a fibrous surface will appear fuzzy and unclear in design.

The detail of the rug in Plate 51 shows another method of macramé. This one is done with the double half-hitch knot. A heavy (½") rope forms the base or holding cord for the knots. Plain and dyed jute are used for the wrapping cords that are half-hitched over the rope. The ½-inch rope is cut to the length you want the finished rug to be, including fringe. Attach your wrapping cords onto the

44

50. Macramé rug detail—
the macramé knots show clearly in
the smooth but hard-finished rope.

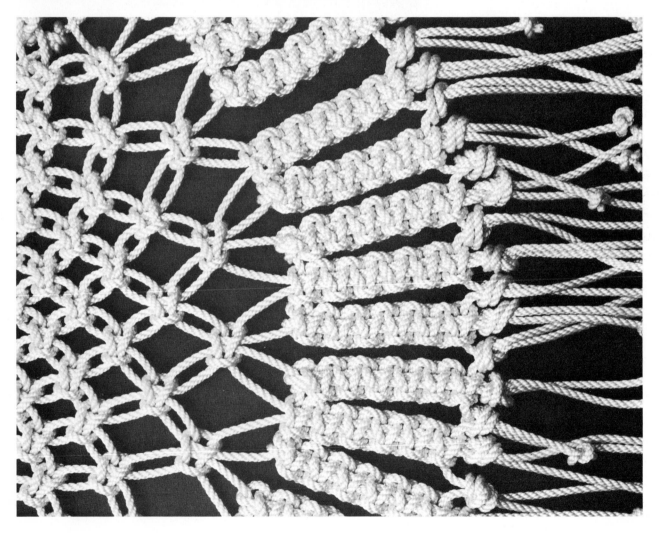

first length of rope in grouped colors to make a varied, striped design. Leave about 3 inches at each end of the rope for fringe. The wrapping cords should be cut about eight times the width of the finished rug. If the rug is going to be 2 feet wide, cut your wrapping cord 16 feet long. Find the middle of each cord and attach it at that point to the first piece of rope. This leaves you 8 feet of cord with which to work. If you find it too long to handle easily, roll it up and secure it with a rubber band so you can release the cord as you need it. After each piece of rope is wrapped and knotted with the jute, add an-

other length of rope and half hitch over that. Your rug will grow in ½-inch bands. A rug 2 feet wide by 3 feet long will use approximately 45 pieces of rope, each three feet long, or a total of 135 feet of rope. When you have attached the last length of rope, cut the jute cords so they are an extra 2 inches long. Turn the rug over and weave the jute ends back into the rug to finish. Ravel the 3 inches of rope on each end of the rug to form the fringe.

The rug shown in Plate 52 is also made with a base of rope and is used on a counter under small potted plants. The rope used

51. Macramé rug detail by Rebecca Biller—jute fibers are half-hitched over rope in another variation of macramé.

52. "Wrapped Rope Rug" 15x18″ (left)
by Joyce Aiken. Coils of various colors
are placed together, then joined by stitching.

53. Wrapped sisal detail—yarn is wrapped
round and round sisal to form a solid color cord.

54. As wrapped sections are finished,
they are joined to other coils.

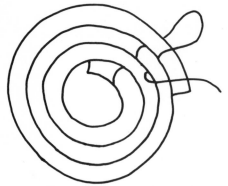

55. Coils are sewn together using needle and yarn to weave in and out of coils.

here is sisal wrapped with colored yarns. Pieces of sisal approximately 3 feet long are cut. Each sisal length is then wrapped with a single color of yarn, as seen in Plate 53, and the ends secured with white glue. After all the ropes are wrapped, some are coiled to lie flat. With a yarn needle and matching yarn, stitch the coils together with a weaving stitch as in Drawing 55. Other wrapped ropes are laid in place to connect one coil to another as in Plate 54. When the design pleases you, the rope and coils are stitched down with carpet thread to a heavy, dark colored upholstery fabric. After all the rope is sewn in place, the fabric is cut from around the outside edge of the rug. The latex coating on the back of the upholstery fabric keeps it from fraying so that hemming is unnecessary.

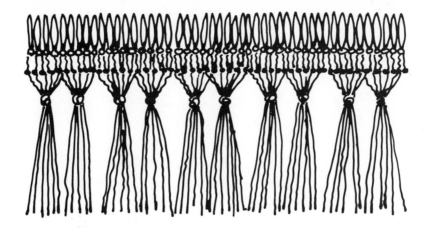

6

JUTE AND BURLAP RUGS

In our world of chrome and glass and polished surfaces we sometimes feel the need for a material that is natural, earthy, easy to live with—yet complementary to the polish around us. Weathered wood gives that warmth to walls. Burlap lends natural quality to floors. Burlap is a fabric made of jute fibers. It is coarsely woven and we often think of it as gunny sack material. Now it can be bought by the yard in natural grey-brown or in brightly dyed colors. For making a rug, natural undyed burlap is more satisfactory. Dyed burlap often has rayon threads woven in that tend to break easily when handled. The natural colored fabric comes in many widths. Choose a width that is right for the finished rug so that the selvage forms the sides and can be left unhemmed. Turn the

end pieces of the burlap under about ¾ inch and machine or hand-stitch to hold the threads in place.

The burlap can be decorated by taking away some of its threads and by adding others. The rug in Plate 56 and Color Plate 10 is made of natural burlap with natural colored jute twine in browns, red-browns, and off-white—all blending together to make an area rug in varied textures and warm colors.

Yarns, instead of jute, can also be used with the burlap backing. The rug in Plate 58 has been decorated with wool rug yarns. A wide range of natural or earth colors is available to complement the natural burlap. Because burlap is a lightweight fabric, it will feel and look more rug-like if you put a foam rug pad under it or back it with several layers

49

56. Jute Rug 36x76″ by Susan Morrison. Jute twines are looped, latched and stitched flat in this rug of natural fibers and colors.

of fabric. This rug, shown in progress, employs most of the techniques described in this chapter.

Any of the following techniques can be used in different combinations to decorate your rug:

Pulled Threads. About ½ inch from the selvage on one side, carefully cut two or more of the threads running across the fabric. With a blunt yarn needle unweave them until you can hold the threads in your fingers. Gently pull each until that pulled thread can be identified at the opposite end of the fabric. When you are sure which threads are being pulled, carefully cut those same threads ½ inch from the opposite selvage. Now pull the threads out of the weave. Save them to put back into the rug later on if you desire. Removal of the pulled threads leaves an open area. New yarns or jute may now be woven back into those open areas. Choose yarn

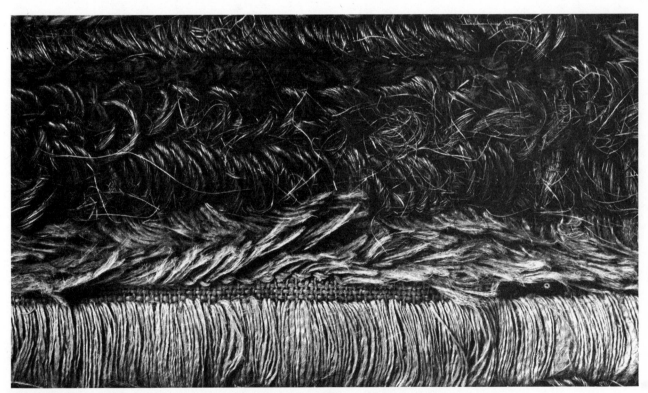

57. Jute rug detail—looped jute and latch knotting show above a row of stitching, with the texture of the jute appearing between them.

heavier than the threads you have removed and weave across the burlap as shown in Plate 59. Try simple weaving of over one thread, under one thread or over two threads, under two threads, or other combinations.

Rya. With jute or yarn, use the rya method explained in Chapter 13 for adding looped threads to the rug. Keep the design in bands going across the rug and vary the length of the loops on different bands.

Sewing. Decide on the width of a sewn band. Those from ½ to 2 inches wide are easiest to handle. Sew across the top of the fabric, through, under and back up so that you have a solid band of threads on both top and bottom. This is essentially the same as a satin stitch. The coarse weave of the burlap allows you to easily keep the threads even.

Plate 57 shows a detail of the various techniques discussed. The combination of flat sewing, raised loops and cut yarns creates a rug rich in textured variations.

59. "Yarn and Burlap" rug detail—the reweaving is shown in progress where a needle draws two strands of yarn through the opened section of burlap.

58. "Yarn and Burlap" rug (opposite)   3′ wide   by Joyce Aiken. Yarns are rewoven into the burlap backing along with sections of satin stitches and knotting.

60. "White Land-
scape" 36x72" by
Darlene Huckobey.
The hills and valleys
on the surface of
this rug result from
changing lengths of
the latched yarns.

61. Latch hook—
a simple but essential
tool for latching.

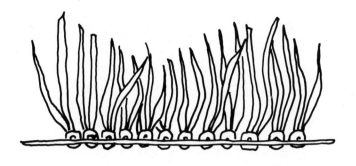

7

LATCHED RUGS

One of the most luxurious of all rug surfaces comes through the process of latching. Yarns of various weights and lengths can be combined for a sculptural effect, giving a thick, lush pile. The latched rug shown in the frontispiece, Plate 1, and opposite in Plate 60 is one which would be as much at home on the wall as on the floor. Either way, it invites one to run fingers or toes through the deep soft pile.

Some special materials are needed for this type of rug. Drawing 61 shows the latch hook necessary for working in this method. The hook has a small latch which swings freely to open or close the hook end. The hook is pushed under a thread and up through the adjacent opening in the grid until the latch is clear of the thread. A piece of thread is slipped over the handle and down the shaft toward the latch. The ends of the yarn are put into the hook opening and the latch is

closed over them as in Plate 62. Now the hook is pulled back and out of the grid. This pulls the yarn ends through the loop first wrapped around the handle, and securely knots them. All the yarn is put in the rug in this manner. Each piece of yarn should be about ½-inch longer than two times the desired length of the pile height. A 2-inch piece of yarn will knot and stand up about ¾ of an inch. For areas where it is desirable to have all the same height, cut the yarn with the use of a gauge.

"White Landscape" shows the possibilities for doing sculptural surfaces. Some of the yarns stand only an inch high while other yarns are 8 to 10 inches long. The surface changes become much more important when all of the yarns are one color. White reflects the light so you are more aware of surface changes in the rug than if the rug were a dark color. Other factors that create interest in an

62. Latch hook detail—the hook goes under one of the backing threads then grasps the ends of the yarn to pull them back into a knot.

63. "Red, Red, Red" detail—a combination of clipped felt and latched yarns makes a rich change of texture.

all-one-color rug are different thicknesses and different textures of yarn. When planning a rug like this, divide the rug into areas —narrow and wide or large and small in combinations that are pleasing. Fill these areas with short or long yarns to give the change of height necessary for the sculptural look. Long yarns at each end act as fringe.

Wool rug yarn is one of the best materials for a latched rug. It keeps its twist and springs back in place after being walked on. See Color Plate 8 for a wool yarn rug. Cotton yarns open up at the cut end and tend to matt down. They also hold the dirt while the natural oil in wool yarn resists soiling. The cost of wool will be about three times that of cotton. There are some cotton and rayon yarn blends that are available which are more satisfactory than all-cotton yarn.

The rug in Color Plate 12 uses wool yarns and felt strips. The felt covers about one-fourth of the total rug area and costs a fraction of what the yarn would cost to cover the same area. It stands up higher than the yarn and adds interest to the rug. A combination rug like this one that uses both felt and yarn must be planned so that the felt areas are sewn in first. The felt is cut in 2- to 3-inch strips and sewn by hand or machine down the center of each strip, as described in Chapter 10. The colored areas of yarn are worked around the felt and occasionally in between the strips as seen in Plate 63. There are also some changes in the length of yarn in some areas. Though originally planned for the floor, this rug has always hung on the wall and adds a wonderful splash of color to the room. A 1x2" board is wired to one side of the back of the rug and hung over nails on the wall.

Another latched rug is shown in Plate 70. For the person who "can't draw a straight line", a rug like this one takes advantage of that lack of talent. Long and short cut pile

64. "Blue and Green"   6x9'   by Betty Smith. Though it
resembles a hooked rug, this one is done by a method called latch
hook. It uses a crochet technique to lock in the loops.

58

65. The latch hook is slipped under a grid thread and the yarn is looped over it.

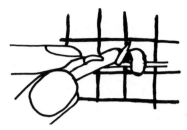

67. The hook remains in the yarn loop but slides over the grid thread to pick up the yarn on the other side.

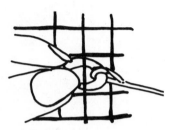

66. The yarn is drawn back by the latch hook, just into the opening in which the hook was first inserted.

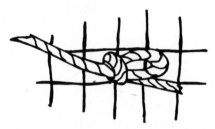

68. This yarn is pulled through to form a loop and knot on the surface.

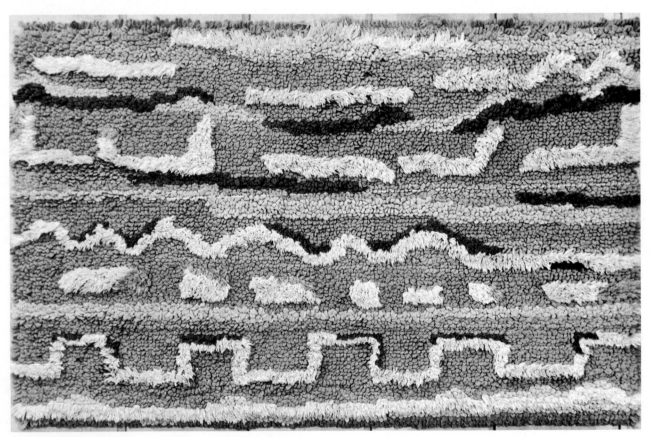

69. "Odds and Ends"   30x45"   by Betty Smith.
A combination of looped yarns and cut pile both result from the latch hook technique.

give a high-low look to the surface.

The rug in Plate 64 also uses latch backing and a latch hook but has the look of a hooked rug. The yarn in this rug is not cut in small lengths. It is a continuous strand and is cut only when another color is introduced. The method of working is basically one of using a crochet stitch. Drawing 65 shows the latch hook slipped under a grid thread and into an open square where it picks up the yarn. The latch closes over the yarn and the hook pulls it back under the grid thread and just up into the square as seen in Drawing 66. The hook remains in the loop but now slides over the top of the grid thread, catches the yarn and pulls it through the loop to form a longer loop that will stand up on the surface. See Draw-ings 67 and 68. You can regulate the length of the loop by inserting a finger from your left hand through the loop and pulling on the strand of yarn until it is tight. Whenever you start a new length of yarn be sure to pull the yarn end to the front of the backing material and clip the same as the loops. When you end a length of yarn pull the last loop a bit longer and cut through it. Pull out the free yarn and your stitch is secure.

If you want a combination of loops and cut yarn, work the stitch as described. Clip some of the loops and leave other areas uncut. Plate 69 shows a rug handled this way. The loops that are to be cut are pulled longer than the uncut loop so there is an interesting change of surface levels of the yarns.

70. "Kristi's Rug" 3x5' by Jackie Vermeer.
Wavy bands of color are latched with yarns of different lengths giving a high-low pattern to this rug.

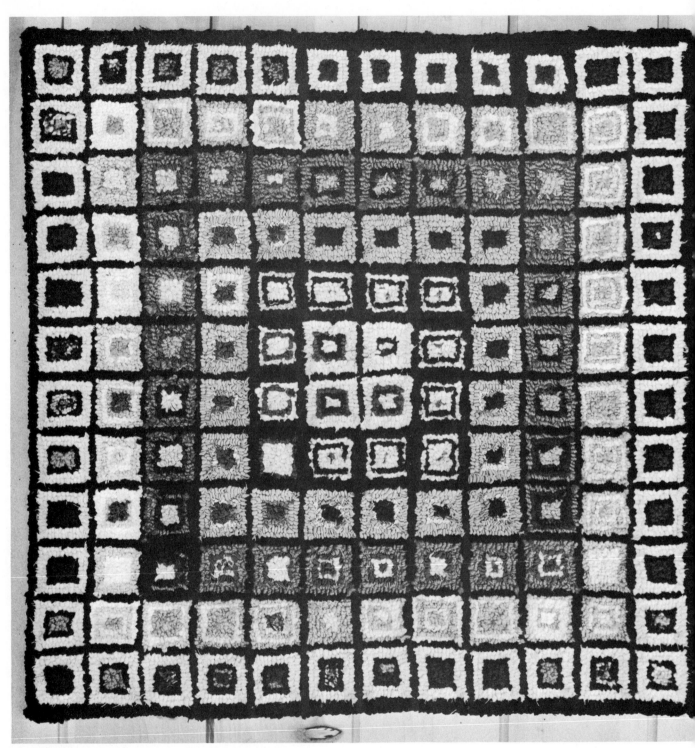

71. "City Blocks"   3x3'   by Norma Gibbs.
The slight variations from one square to the next give
this traditional hooked rug a contemporary feeling.

8

HOOKED RUGS

Almost every family has had a hooked rug in its possession at one time or another. Many of these rugs, made by a grandmother or an aunt, are still in use and show little wear. The hooked rugs that our grand-mothers made utilized worn-out woolen clothes that no longer could be cut down or made over for another family member. Every scrap of wool was kept for a rug or quilt.

The traditional rag rug as seen in Plate 71 needs no expensive equipment or material. The woolens saved from worn-out clothes, a burlap bag from grain or potatoes, a wooden frame and a hook are all you need to make a warm and durable rug. The process is a simple one.

Small rugs can be hooked in your lap. Larger rugs are much easier to work if they are stretched over a wooden frame made of 1x2" pine. Almost any sturdy frame made of wood that you might have around the house will work if you do not want to construct your own. Tack the burlap in place on the frame with thumb tacks or lace it on with heavy twine. The burlap must be held taut so it does not stretch as you work on it.

The design is drawn directly onto the front side of the burlap with a crayon and all hook-

72. "City Blocks" detail—straight lines
of hooking at the edges of the squares produce
rows of single loops, contrasting to
the random-placed loops at the corners.

73. "City Blocks" detail—
when hooking is finished, the edges
are turned back and hemmed.

ing is done from the front. The outlines of an area are hooked first and then filled in. Plate 74 shows the burlap backing with the hook pulling a strip of wool up through the weave. The wool is cut according to its weight and a dress-weight wool would be cut into ¼-inch strips. One hand holds the hook and the other hand guides the wool on the under side of the burlap. The end pieces of the wool strip are pulled through to the front of the burlap and left about 1 inch long. They will be trimmed back to the height of the surrounding loops later. The loops can vary in length with most of them about ⅜ inch high. Pull a loop up through the burlap with the hook. Move two threads away and pull up another loop. You can work at random with loops going in all directions or in rows where each loop is carefully turned to follow the next one to it. This creates a more formal pattern. The detail in Plate 72 shows formal rows of hooking that enclose areas of random loops. The hooking can be random or formal but the stitches should not cross over each other on the back. These places wear faster than the rest of the rug. When all the rug has been hooked, go back and clip the loose strip ends back to the loop height. Remove from the frame and trim the edge of the burlap to 2 inches. Turn the rug over, pin the edging as in Plate 73 and hem.

Another method of hooking has become popular in the last few years—using yarn instead of rags. It is less trouble but more expensive than saving, washing, and cutting **wool scraps. Color Plate 3 shows a hooked rug made by using yarns.** You need a burlap backing, a frame, a punch needle and yarn. With this rug you work from the back of the rug and push a needle holding yarn through the burlap to the front. The needle is threaded with yarn through a hole close to the handle, up a groove, and into a hole at the end of the needle. You hold onto this end of the yarn and push the needle through the burlap. Carefully withdraw the point of the needle and move about two threads away and push into the burlap again as shown in Plate 76. Each time you do this you leave another loop of yarn on the front of the rug. See Plate 75. With a little practice, your loops will attain a consistent height. Most dime stores carry inexpensive punch needles. A more expensive needle, available in yarn shops, has an attachment that allows you to regulate the length of the loops. With this needle, you can design so that some of the areas in the rug are higher looped than others. Plate 77 and Color Plate 13 show a rug that has been handled this way. This rug is framed with a metal edge and hangs on the wall.

The rug in Plate 78 was designed according to the wishes of a six-year-old boy. It depicts a space ship along with the earth, the moon and another planet. The boy's name is a prominent part of the design—red letters on a bright blue sky. Hooking makes possible designs of a somewhat personal nature. Children's drawings can be easily adapted for hooking. Commemorative rugs, giving dates, names and events are marvelous for weddings, birthdays, housewarmings, and special celebrations and holidays.

You will want to consider dye lots of yarn if you need large areas of solid colors in your rug. Take care to buy the same dye lot of one color for these areas. It is difficult to know how much burlap each kind of yarn will cover

74. Rug hook—narrow strips of cloth are pulled through the burlap backing in the first stage of a hooked rug.

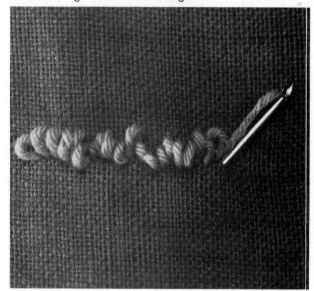

75. Yarn hooking detail—loops of the yarn come through on the facing side which will be the top of the rug.

76. Hooking with yarn, from the back side, the hook moves in a continuous line along the burlap.

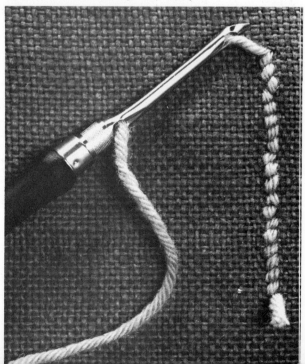

78. "David's Rug" 3x5' by Jackie Vermeer. Children's ideas
or drawings can readily be adapted to hooking as seen
in this rug depicting a boy's interest in the moon landing.

"Mrs. McKenzie's Garden"
6x54" by Jean Ray Laury. Layers
f felt are stacked, one on top
f another, then areas are cut away
reveal the colors beneath.

2. "Pedestals" 36x40"
by Jean Ray Laury. Bands
of colored felt, cut with
decorative edges, are machine
appliquéd in this felt rug.

3. "Hand Hooked Rug" by Gere Kavanaugh. Hand hooking makes possible the line detail and intricate pattern in this bed of flowers. (Courtesy California Design/Nine.)

4. "Crimson Bouquet"   30x36"   by Jean Ray Laury. French knots attach stacks of flower cutouts in this contemporary version of the old-fashioned button rug.

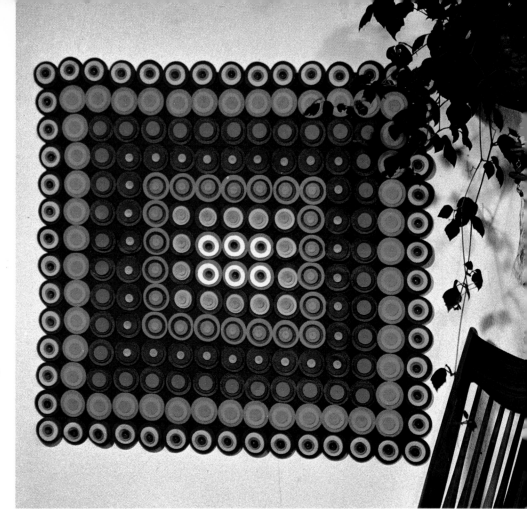

5. "The Squares"   34x34" by Jean
Ray Laury. Precut circles of felt
are stacked and then sewn to a backing
in this variation of a button rug.

6. "Egyptian Desert"   30x50"
by Ethel Jane Beitler. A
rich array of golds forms this
deceptively simple design in
a yarn-hooked wall hanging.

7. "Green Shingles" 3x5' by Joyce Aiken. Felt strips spaced in overlapping layers are alternated with latched red yarn.

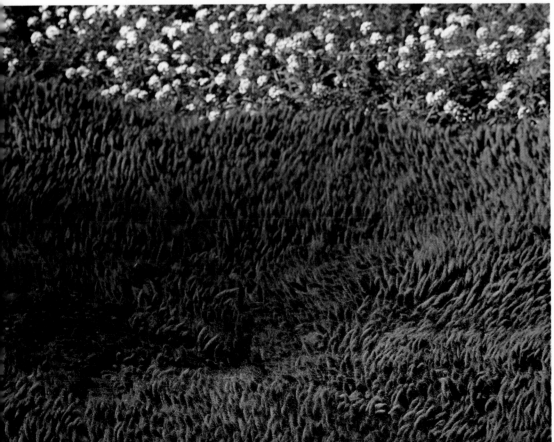

8. Green Yarn Rug 4x6' by Francesca Trynauer. Red and green yarns resemble a field of scattered flowers in this wool rug. (Courtesy California Design/Nine.)

9. "Green Grow the Flowers Oh" 3′ diameter by Jean Ray Laury. Assorted pinks and greens are machine-appliquéd to a double thick layer of white felt.

10. Jute Rug 36x72″ by Susan Morrison. The soft, warm colors of this rug result from the use of natural jute and burlap.

11. "Blue River" 3x6' by Jean Ray Laury. Long strips of felt are machine-stitched so close to one another that the edges of felt stand upright.

12. "Red, Red, Red" 4x6' by Darlene Huckobey. Felts and yarns are used in this combination of latch and strip rug techniques.

13. ''Seed Pod''   21x28''   by Jerrie
Peters. High and low hooking
accent this chrome-framed panel.

14. ''Rag Bag Oval''   18x30''   by
Jenny Stukenborg. This soft-colored
rug is made with rag fringe,
using a simple-to-make string loom.

15. "Stars and Stripes" 40x58" by Joyce Aiken. Hand-sewn running stitches apply red and white blocks to a solid blue background.

16. "Queen of Diamonds" by Terry Van Buren. A playing card inspired this brilliantly colored hooked rug.

79. "Burning Bush"   30x50"   by Ethel Jane Beitler.
Metal hooks are attached at the top of this panel so that a
rod can be used to support its weight in hanging.

80. "The Forest" 36x60" by Ethel Jane Beitler. Hooked rugs or panels need not be limited to a rectangular shape. This one, rounded at the corners, has an angular base offset with three large tassels.

before working out your own sample gauge. As a rule, a 70-yard skein of medium weight yarn will cover about 36 square inches or a 6-inch square. Most yarn stores or department stores will allow you to buy plenty of yarn and return to them what you do not use. It is safer to do this than to run out of yarn before you have finished your rug.

As you are working, if you find an area that is not right, you can remove the loops from the rug by pulling the yarn lines out from the back. This makes it easy to change your design as you are working, but it also means that a pull on a loop by a playful cat or an inquisitive child can just as easily remove a section of your rug. To protect your rug from this kind of accident, you should paint latex adhesive on the back of the finished rug to lock in all of the loops. Wall-hung rugs do not need this kind of protection. "Burning Bush" in Plate 79 and "The Forest" in Plate 80 were designed to be hung on the wall. Each has a row of metal rings sewn to the top edge. A metal or wooden rod slips through the rings and is suspended on the wall by nails or hooks.

Plate 81 shows a hearth rug made from a combination of felt pieces and yarn-hooked areas. Felt bands are placed on the burlap backing in an arrangement that leaves bands of burlap exposed. Sew the felt onto the backing by hand with stitches about 1/8 of an inch from the edges of the felt. Now you can hook in the burlap areas. Because the felt keeps the burlap from stretching, it is necessary to tack only the larger rugs to a frame when working this way. Only the areas that have been hooked need to have a latex coating. The combination of felt and hooked yarn gives a pleasing high-low look to the surface as seen in Plate 82.

Two stunning examples of rug hooking, both used as wall hangings, can be seen in Color Plates 6 and 16.

81. "Sticks and Stones"   2x3'   by Joyce Aiken. Bands of felt
are sewn to the burlap backing to alternate with the areas of hooking.

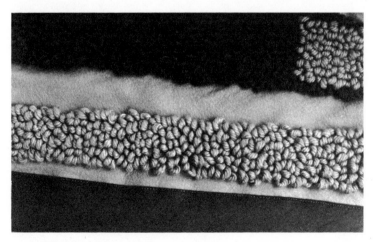

82. "Sticks and Stones" detail—areas
of the burlap are covered with bands of
felt in one color, then a second color
can be machine-sewn over the first giving
more firmness and strength to the rug.

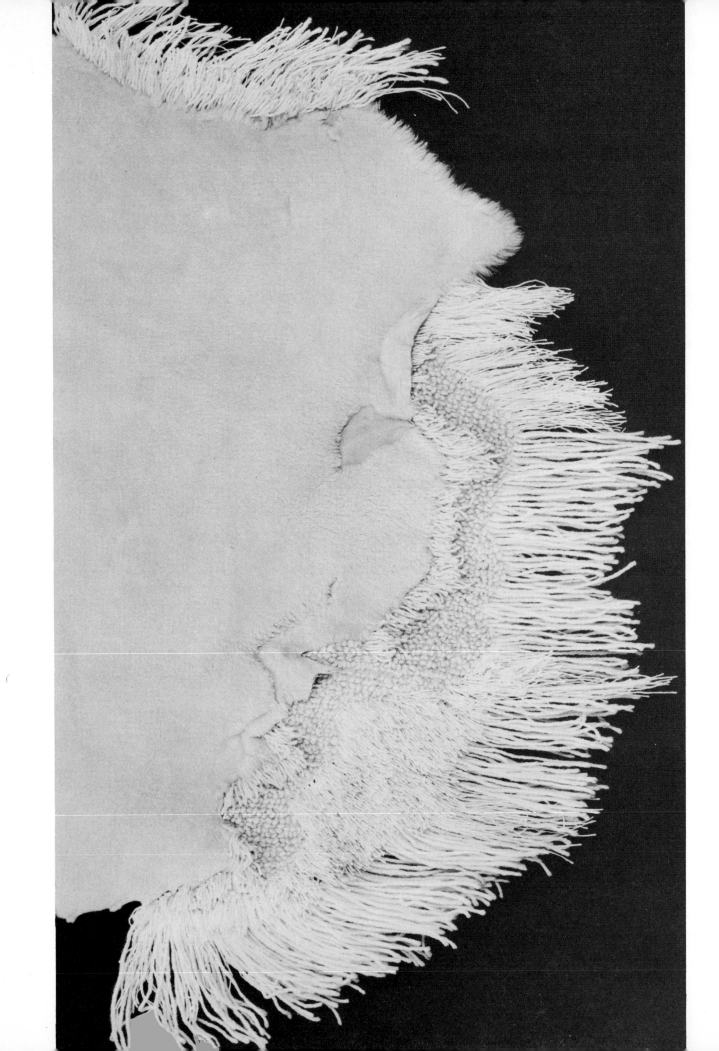

9

FUR AND YARN RUGS

A rug that combines more than one texture offers a visual as well as a tactile experience —an invitation for your hands and feet to run over the surface. The fur and yarn rug takes its place naturally next to the "get up" side of the bed where your bare feet can start the day feeling good, or in front of a fireplace where you can sit and let your hands investigate the texture.

The materials needed for this method of rug making include latch backing, a fur skin, various yarns, a strong needle, thread and a latch hook. There are numerous leather or hobby shops in most urban areas that provide a variety of suitable skins. Lamb skins are especially nice and can be found in long or short wool. If you choose short wool, it will be easier to hook or latch around the fur. Skins that are classed as "seconds" are often the most desirable; they allow you to work yarns into the ragged areas or into those holes in the fur that make the skin imperfect. Plate 85 shows fur, latch hook and yarn as it has been latched into the backing. The cost of these imperfect furs will be about one-third the cost of perfect skins.

When you have chosen a skin, decide whether it needs yarn worked on all around it or if it should have yarn added to just a part of it. In Plate 83 the rug is worked on only two areas. Use a strong needle and carpet thread and stitch around the edge but inside the fur area so that the thread does not show. If you are adding yarn to just a section of the edge, sew the latch backing to that area and cut it for the amount of latching you are going to do. Now look at the skin and see which direction the fur grows at the edges. Choose thin yarns for latching close to the skin if you want the feeling of the fur growing to con-

3. "Igloo Robe" 30x45" by Joyce Aiken. Soft fur combines with yarns and fringe to make an inviting surface.

69

tinue into the rest of the rug. You may want to latch hook next to the skin in some areas for contrast as in Plate 84. Chapter 7 explains how to latch and latch hook.

As the yarn part of the rug develops, you will begin to feel in tune with the fur and the decisions on sizes of yarn and whether to hook or latch seem to come naturally. Plate 86 shows a rectangular rug with yarn worked around the skin. The yarns latched on each end are about 8 inches long and act as a fringe. When you have finished the rug you will want to have achieved a natural combination of fur and yarn.

84. "Igloo Robe" detail—thick and thin yarns are hooked or latched next to a lamb skin to suggest a continuation of the growing fur.

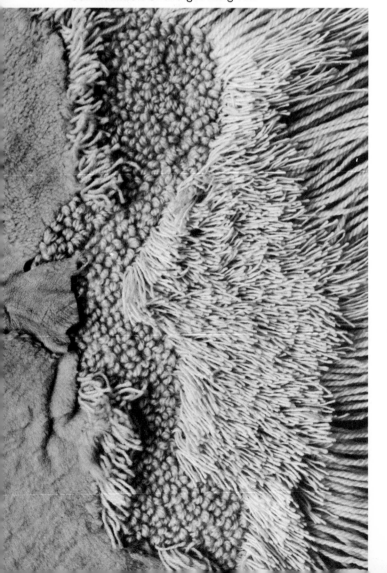

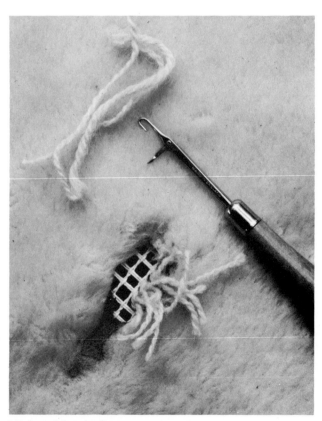

85. Latching in fur—yarns are latched in open or damaged areas of the skin.

86. ''Fur Sleeping''   3x5'   by Joyce Aiken. A baby lamb skin,
framed by white yarns, is set off with a deep thick fringe, also of white.

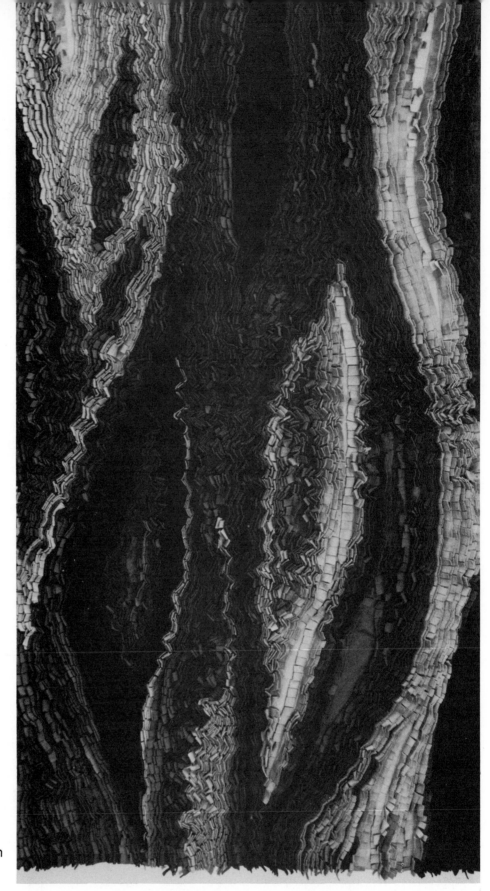

87. "Blue River" 3x6'
by Jean Ray Laury.
Strips of felt, sewn
down the center, are then
clipped to make
this thick shag effect.

10

STRIP RUGS

The versatility of felt as a material for rug making is surprisingly unlimited. Because of its nonwoven quality we are able to handle it quite differently from other materials. Cut edges do not fray or ravel.

Color Plate 11 and Plate 87 show a 3x6′ felt rug that uses the edges of the felt for the pile or shag. To make this type of rug, decide on the thickness or height you want in the felt. A 1-inch-thick rug needs strips of felt 2 inches wide. The technique is a simple one. Determine the size of your rug and choose a backing for it—like canvas or heavy upholstery fabric that does not stretch. Cut the strips of felt with scissors in approximately the width you need. Do not be too concerned about having your strips exactly even. There is a pleasing quality about the slightly irregular cut of the strips.

The technique for sewing strips to the backing is seen in Plate 88. A strip of the felt is placed on the backing and machine-stitched down the center of the strip. Another strip is sewn about ¼ to ½ inch from the first. As more strips are added to the backing the strips begin to stand up. When all the strips are added to the backing they can be clipped as in Plate 89. This makes the felt more fluid as the clipped pieces fall to one side or the other. Do not clip until all the sewing is finished or you will find it difficult to add a strip next to

the cut one, since the cut strips fall in the path of the sewing machine. The rug in Plate 87 has been sewn in a pattern of flowing lines the length of the backing. You might find your first rug easier to handle if you sew the strips in straight lines across the width of the rug.

Another method of sewing strips to the backing is shown in Plate 90. The edge, rather than the center of the felt, is sewn across the width of a latch backing. Each strip is placed about ¼ to ½ inch from the one next to it. When all of the felt has been sewn, yarn is cut and latched between some of the rows of felt as seen in Plate 91. After the felt has been clipped, the overlapping rows resemble shingles. Plate 93 and Color Plate 7 show a completed rug using this method. The strips extend about three inches beyond the backing on each side and give a loose ruffled look to the edge. Plate 92 shows how the strips look when some are left uncut, some cut, and where yarn has been introduced into some areas. These strips were sewn down the center. Felt handled this way is surprisingly durable and soil-resistant. About the only problem you will have is lint or dust that will need to be shaken out. When the dog has slept too long or hard on the rug, put it in the dryer set on cool and toss for a couple of minutes to make your rug look like new again.

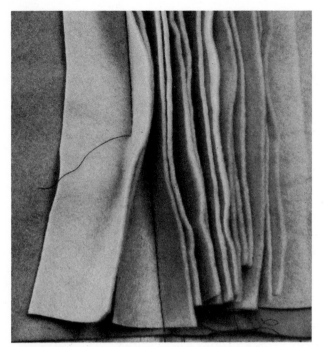

88. Felt strips detail—strips are machine-stitched, each one close to the last.

89. After the strips are sewn, they are clipped to form a fringe.

90. Strips of felt, sewn at one edge rather than in the center, give an overlapping effect.

91. Yarns can be latched between rows of sewn felt.

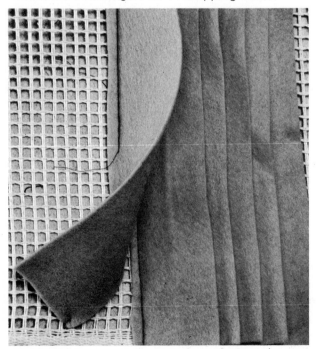

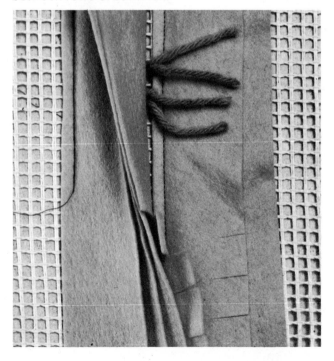

92. Felt strips detail—uncut felt
strips, clipped felt, and latched wool yarn
combine in a rich textural surface.

93. "Green Shingles"   3x5'   by Joyce Aiken.
The rich, thick surface of this rug results from the
overlapping layers of clipped felt and yarns.

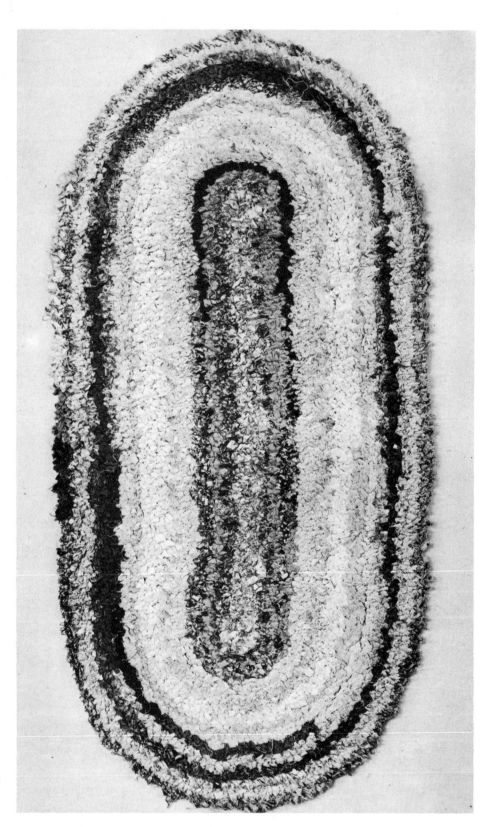

94. "Rag Bag Oval"
18x30"   by
Jenny Stukenborg.
Short pieces of rag
strips were knotted on the
string loom in this rug
made about 40 years ago.

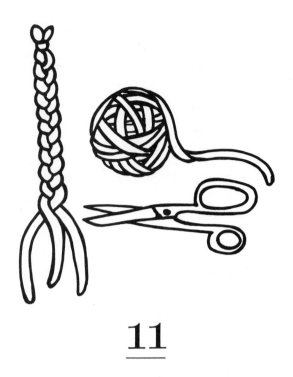

11

RAG RUGS

For the person who finds it difficult to part even with outdated clothing, rag rugs may be the answer for putting wool or cotton scraps to use. Not only is it more efficient, but it is also more attractive to have a rag rug on the floor than to have the bag of scraps in the closet. Some rag rugs use large pieces of fabrics cut or torn in strips.

The knotted rag rug in Plate 94 and in Color Plate 14 is made of short narrow pieces of cotton fabric not ordinarily used for rugs. It even makes use of the sock or glove that lost its mate. Plate 95 shows the simple loom needed for making this rug. This one is made of two pieces of driftwood, though yours could be made with regular boards. Use 1 inch thick wood; the base is approximately 6 inches wide and 16 inches long, and the upright is 4 inches high and 6 inches wide.

Place the upright on the base about 5 inches from one end. Fasten the upright from underneath the base with long screws or nails.

Drawing 98 shows a loom with two long nails in the short section positioned so that two spools of string can slip over them. A third long nail is placed at the opposite end of the board. On top of the upright board are two pairs of nails to hold the string taut. To warp the loom, wrap the string from each spool around the pair of nails in a figure eight leaving enough string to extend down to the nail at the far end. Tie the string around the nail and your loom is ready. The string is the warp of the loom.

For a 1-inch-thick rug you will want strips of cotton about ½ inch wide and 2½ inches long. To make all the strips the same length first tear your fabric in long strips that are

95. String loom by Bea Slater.
Driftwood makes this simple string loom as
beautiful as it is functional. The string
warp is in place and the tying is underway.

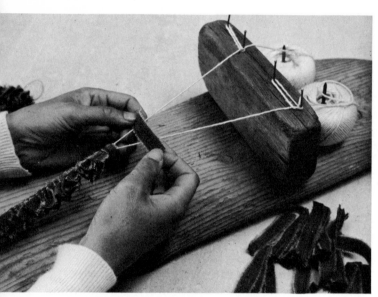

96. Placed over the warp strings,
a denim strip is readied for tying.

97. The strip is brought around the strings,
down, and back up through the center.

½ inch wide. Wrap these around a gauge in a single layer. A gauge can be made with a piece of cardboard 2½ inches wide and at least 8 inches long. Fold the cardboard down the center and wrap with the ½ inch wide cloth. Drawing 99 shows the gauge with the point of the scissors slipped into the folded cardboard and ready to cut the strips all the same length.

Knotting is done by placing one of these strips of fabric over the warp threads as in Plate 96. Then wrap the ends over the warp as shown in Plate 97. Pull the ends up between the warp, as in Drawing 100. Slide the knotted fabric strip down the warp threads to the nail. Continue to knot each piece of fabric, sliding them down tight until the warp threads are full. Lift the string off the end nail and loosen the warp threads from around the pair of nails in the upright wood. Draw a new length of string from each spool, slip the last knotted fabric strip over the end nail and tighten the warp strings on the nails at the upright. Continue knotting as before. You will have a continuous strip of knotted fringe that can be sewn together when it is a few feet long. It is easy to work for a while making fringe, alternating that with coiling and sewing. Do not break the warp string until you have the rug as large as you like. When the last knot is tied, cut the warp threads and tie behind the last knot. The fringe is coiled clockwise in an oval or round shape and whipped together on the back with strong linen or cotton thread. The proportion of the oval is determined by the length of the center strip. To determine this, subtract the desired finished width from the length, and the difference tells you the length of the initial center strip. If you want an oval rug 20 inches wide and 36 inches long, you subtract 20 from 36 and make your center strip 16 inches long. Ease the fringe on the curves so the rug will lie flat.

An effect similar to that of the braided rug is one that uses a process of weaving the fabric strip around two base strips. This is a good way to make your wool rags go further. If you want the look of a braided rug, but do not have enough wool rags, consider working with this method. Collect your wool scraps, but you will also need men's old cotton or denim pants material. Tear the denim in 2-inch strips and the wool in 1-inch strips. Fold the denim strip in half and hand sew an end of wool strip to the denim at the fold. Drawing 101 shows the wool sewn to the denim and the first wrap around the denim strip. Fold the wool strip down the center so that you are working with a double ½-inch strip. Plates 106 and 107 show the way the wool is woven around the denim. Each time you wrap with the wool be sure to cover the edges of the strip above it. As the denim and wool strips are used up, sew new strips onto them. A bias seam makes the nicest and least noticeable connection as shown in Drawing 102. This method of rug making gives you a solid color braid rather than the multi-colored braid most often seen in the traditional braided rug. Because of the denim core, the woven braid is a very durable rug. When you have made a few feet of the woven braid you can start to coil it for a round or oval rug. Whip it together on the back with strong thread. Determine the oval shape as explained in this chapter for the knotted shag rug. To finish the rug, cut the last 12 inches of denim core strip gradually narrower so the braid becomes smaller and works in close with the braid next to it.

As already mentioned, the traditional braided rug is often multi-colored. Plate 108 shows a 7x9' oval rug braided with many colors of wool strips. Much of the same information concerning the woven braid applies here. Cut or tear strips of fabric, cotton or wool, 2½ to 3½ inches wide and as long as

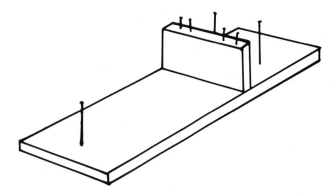

98. This simple loom is made with two pieces of 1" lumber—6x16" for the bottom piece; 6x4" for the upright.

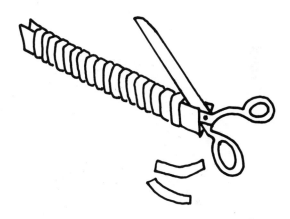

99. A folded cardboard makes a simple cutting edge. The blade of the scissors slips into the open edge of the fold.

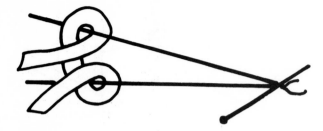

100. Tying on to the warp strings—
a short strip of fabric placed
over the warp threads is drawn back up
through the center to secure it.

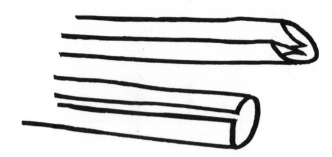

103. Folding the fabric—the raw edges
of material can be folded in so that
no frayed areas show on top of the rug.

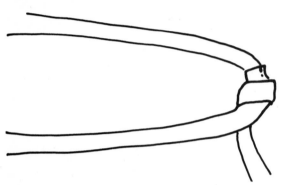

101. Tying for a wrapped braid—
a strip of wool fabric is stitched to a
strip of denim, forming a T. Then the
wool is wrapped once around the denim.

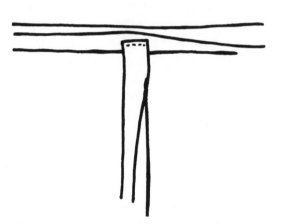

104. Starting the braid—the third
strip needed for a braid is stitched in
place to hold it secure for braiding.

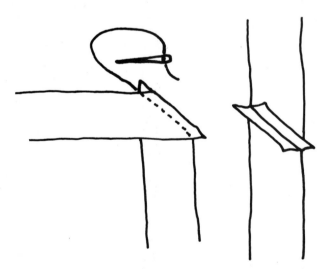

102. Joining strips—a bias seam
makes a smooth way of joining strips.

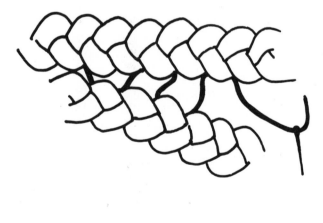

105. Joining braids—the finished
rows of braids are joined together with
double carpet thread or with string.

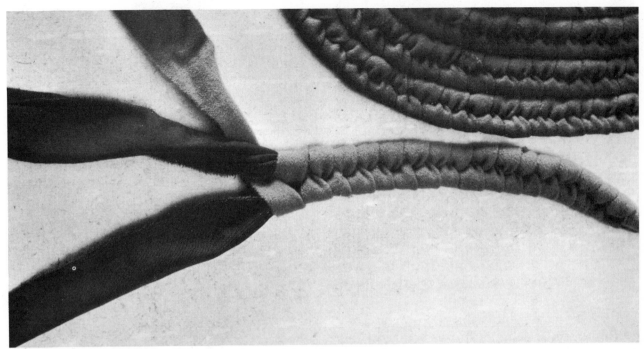

106. Wrapped braid detail—A length of wool fabric is wrapped around the right hand denim strip and then under the left denim strip.

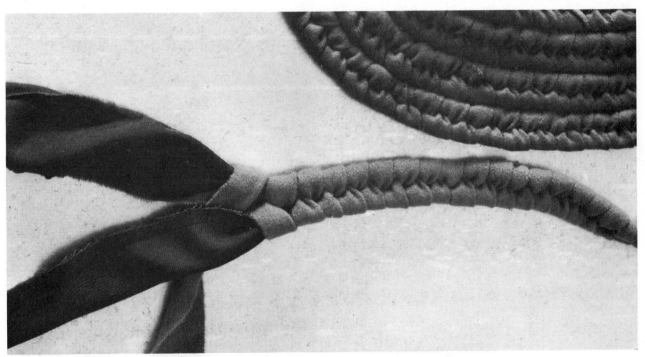

107. The wool is wrapped over the left hand denim strip and then back to the right in a continuous wrapping that leaves a wool surfaced rug with a denim core.

possible. Fold the strips so the outside edges come together in the center of the wrong side of the fabric. Now bring the folded edges together to make a neat flat strand. These steps are seen in Drawing 103. Keep these strands folded with the help of pins or carefully roll them into coils. To start a three-color braid unfold the ends of two strips and sew the ends together with a bias seam. After joining, fold as before with raw edges of seam hidden. Attach the third folded strip to form a T as in Drawing 104. Start your braid by folding the right strand over the center strand and then the left strand over that. Continue while keeping the folded edges toward the center of the braid. As a strand ends, attach a new one with a bias seam.

It is best to assemble the rug as you continue to braid. Lacing is the easiest and the strongest way of connecting the braids. A blunt needle, threaded with double strands of carpet thread or string, is drawn through the loop of one braid and then through the loop of the braid opposite, as shown in Drawing 105. Ease in the fullness on the curves to keep the work flat. It may be necessary to lace through one loop on the inner braid and through two loops on the outer braid. As you approach the last 15 to 20 inches of the rug, start cutting the strips narrower. This will diminish the size of the braid so that it will blend gradually into the last braided row of the rug.

108. "Braided Rug" 7x9' by Jackie Vermeer. This traditional braided rug alternates dark and light colors for an all over multi-colored effect.

109. Hoop rug—the authors are shown tying
in extra warp strips on a large hoop rug.

13

RYA RUGS

The Rya rug is a luxurious addition to any home whether it is used as a rug, wall hanging or pillow cover. The long pile uses more yarn than most other methods so a large Rya rug may be expensive to make. Leftover skeins or balls of yarn from knitting or weaving can be incorporated into any Rya rug. They can be combined with specially selected colors and will help offset the investment in new yarns.

The Rya method of rug making is a simple one. You need a large-weave backing material like burlap or homespun. There are special backings available, made especially for Rya, that have strips of close weave alternat-

ing with strips of open weave.

The floor pillow in Plate 120 has been knotted on a homespun fabric. The method of knotting is shown in Drawing 122. Thread a large needle with a piece of yarn a length you can easily handle. Work on the face side of the rug backing. Start at the left hand edge of the backing, pointing the needle toward the left. Sew under two warp threads leaving the end of the yarn at least 2 inches long. Cross over to the right 5 or 6 warp threads. Then repeat the first step, by sewing under two warp threads. This completes the knot and a loop must be left in the yarn before making the next knot. This loop will be cut

120. "Cliney's Pillow"   3x4'   by Gayle Smalley. This thick, luxurious floor pillow, made for a favorite pet dog, would invite man or beast to relax and enjoy an afternoon's nap.

91

later to form the pile. The rug may be continued in this manner. It is sometimes difficult to keep the loops a consistent length and, if you wish the rug to have an even pile, a pile gauge is helpful. Drawing 123 shows the yarn being knotted over a pile gauge. After each knot is completed the yarn is slipped under the gauge, up over the top and down to the backing for the next knot. After a row of knots is completed a pair of scissors is slipped under the loop and across the top of the gauge and the yarn is cut.

Much of the appeal of the Rya rugs is the combination of various fibers and weights of yarns. The detail in Plate 121 shows a range of sizes from small thread-like yarns to heavy rug yarns. The finished rug is shown in Plate 124. The result is a richness of both surface texture and color. A collection of leftover yarns from other projects can be added to those you have purchased. To estimate the amount of yarn necessary, plan on using 5 pounds of yarn for a 3x4' rug with a 2-inch pile. To make the rug more interesting in design be sure to group some of the yarns in color areas. The pattern that results is more pleasing than if all the different colors were evenly distributed throughout the rug.

The rug in Plate 125 has used a white background to frame a design of multi-colored dark yarns. The strong contrast of dark and light is softened by the overlapping of yarn strands.

121. Rya Rug detail—the surface pattern is enriched with the changes in textures, twists and weights of yarn.

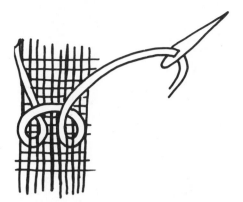

122. Rya Knot—working towards the left, the needle picks up two threads, crosses to the right over six, and picks up two more threads to make this knot.

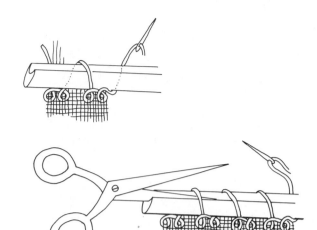

123. Rya Gauge—after the yarn is first knotted, it is wrapped over a pile gauge and knotted again. When a row of knots is completed, use scissors to cut the yarn to form the pile.

124. "Rya Rug" 3x4' by Gayle Smalley. A shadow pattern on rocks inspired the design for this large rug.

125. "Tracks" 2x3′ by Jean Ray Laury. Glue precut
yarns, then stitch close together—row after row.

14

PRECUT YARN AND FELT RUGS

Anyone who weaves or knits probably has an abundance of leftover yarns. If you have purchased precut yarns for latching, you may have an assortment of colors on hand.

If your yarns are not precut, however, an easy way to make them the same length is to wrap the yarn over some object and cut the yarn down the center. Plate 126 shows how. First, you determine the length you want your precut yarns to be; then select the object that will give you the cut length you need.

You can wrap the yarn around a ruler or yardstick, for example. When you cut along one edge (usually 1 inch wide), you get 2-inch lengths. You also can bend a coat hanger to get two parallel wires spaced the appropriate distance apart; wrap the yarn round and

round and cut along one edge as you did with the ruler. Or you can make a gauge from cardboard as shown in Drawing 99.

Here are some possibilities for making good use of yarn once it is cut. Plate 125 shows yarns stitched to a rug backing. This is accomplished by first squeezing a thin line of white household glue along one edge of the backing; then lay the yarns across the glue and press them in place with your fingers. Do not use too much glue—only enough to hold the yarns lightly in place. If a few come off they can easily be placed back on the strip. Allow the glue to dry, then machine-stitch two lines down the center of the yarn—one on each side of the glue line. See Plate 127. A double row of stitching

95

keeps the yarn lying flat. You can avoid breaking a sewing machine needle if you don't stitch through the hardened glue. Now place a second row of yarns across glue on the backing so that the cut ends overlap slightly. Again machine-stitch on either side of the glue. Continue across until the entire backing is covered with cut yarns.

A second precut yarn rug is shown in Plate 128, alternating bands of felt with the yarn on the rug backing. To work on this rug, start at one end and move up row by row to the other end. First, stitch a row of yarns in place. It will help if you mark the rug backing with chalk or pencil line (use a yardstick) to guide you in sewing. Plate 129 shows how to sew

the first row. Then overlap a felt row and sew in the same way. The rug alternates between yarn and felt to the desired size. In some rows the yarn extends farther than in others. By varying colors of both the yarn and felt, you can effect a change of pace and pattern throughout the rug.

You can make a similar rug with an assortment of leftover fringes and edgings, as well as with yarns. Cotton awning fringe is inexpensive, dyes beautifully, and is easier to handle than precut yarns. The primary purpose in the design of these two rugs, however, is to provide a means of making practical use of leftover yarns.

126. Cutting detail— wrap yarn around a ruler, clip along one edge for strips of even lengths.

127. "Tracks" detail—double lines of machine-stitching
hold yarn strips in place on a felt or fabric background.

128. "Flip Flop"   2x3′   by Jean Ray Laury.
Alternate strips of felt with rows of cut yarn
to make use of yarn and felt remnants.

129. "Flip Flop" detail—place yarns on a felt
strip and machine-stitch to rug backing. Overlap the
first strip of felt and yarns with the next strip.

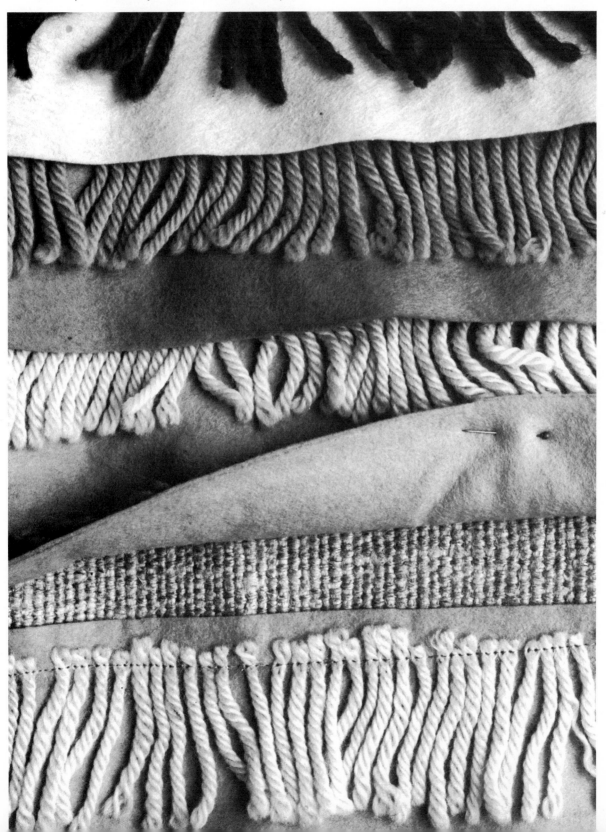

130. "Scroll" 30x45" by Jean Ray Laury. Extend
the life of a worn rug by painting a design on
the back. Fringe dyed blue matches scroll color.

15

CARPET SCRAP RUGS

The past few years have seen a trend to using rug scraps—scraps from carpeting that was put into your home, or pieces purchased from a scrap rug outlet. In any case rug scraps are an easy, inexpensive way to cover and decorate your floors. You can make them look like a patchwork quilt or the most carefully designed custom rug. The number of colors and scraps you have will determine the size of your rug.

Ready-to-use 12-inch squares of carpet cost more than the random-shaped scraps. These squares are marketed as carpeting with instructions to glue them onto the floor with a mastic (thick adhesive for laying linoleum). For a movable rug, glue the squares to any heavy fabric; use latex adhesive which is available in hardware stores. Plate 131 shows a simple but effective use of squares in a checker board pattern of high and low pile carpet.

You have a more difficult design problem when you use random-shaped scraps. First, separate the pieces into similar colors. If there are many different textures in the same color you can make the whole rug of one color with the interest centered on the change of pile. Drawing 132 suggests how random pieces might be put together. You may have to recut some pieces to fit next to others. This is easy if the scraps have a jute or burlap backing that has not been coated with latex. With a crayon or marking pen, draw a line or lines where you want to cut on the burlap. With a sharp mat knife or single-edge razor blade, cut just through the burlap as in Plate 133. Do not try to cut the rug surface. After cutting the burlap, pull the pieces apart and the rug surface will easily separate.

If you use many shapes and colors you will encounter the same design problems as when working with appliqué rugs. Plate 135 shows a rug made from two colors of the same kind of carpet, and designed so that leaf shapes cut from one color exchange and fit into leaf shapes cut from the other color. Special tapes, available from carpet shops, will hold the rug pieces together if you do not want to glue them to a canvas backing.

A small rug that is worn out or is no longer the right color can still be usable if turned over and decorated on the back. The backing

131. Arrange high and low pile carpet squares in a checker board design for the kitchen floor.

132. Glue carpet scraps to a backing in simple straight-line patterns.

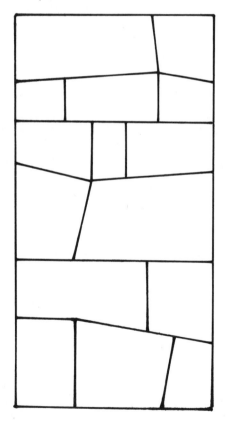

must be uncoated jute or burlap; latex-covered rug backs will not work.

Plate 130 shows a simple rug design that is adapted from a wrought iron gate. You can sketch the design in pencil on the burlap; fill in the design, Plate 134, with a single coat of latex paint. It is important to use latex because it is flexible and will not crack or peel off as the rug is used.

You make the two-color round rug, Plate 136, with pie-shaped wedges of carpet. Make a paper pattern by using a pin on a string attached to a pencil as described in Chapter 1. The length of the string from the center of the circle to the outer edge (the radius) gives you the measure for dividing the circle into six equal parts.

Make a mark on the edge of the circle. Holding the string taut with one end on the mark, use the radius-length string to measure for another mark on the circle's edge. Move the length of string to the next mark and repeat until you have divided the edge of the circle into six parts, with marks an equal distance apart. All lines should go through the center of the circle when you connect the marks opposite each other on the circle.

When your pattern is made, cut it apart into pie-shaped wedges. Using three wedges for each carpet color, draw the pattern on the back of the carpet and cut with a mat knife or razor blade. Alternate the wedges of carpet in color to make the design.

Plates 137 and 138 show further complexities in the same rug, as center sections are cut into small circles, and the colors are again alternated. Use a string and pencil to draw the smaller circles on the back of the rug. After cutting each circle rotate to the next pie-shaped wedge and a new color.

This technique need not be confined to small rugs. A worn-out room-size rug can be turned over and treated in a similar manner, or a large rug with worn areas can be cut up and those parts turned over and painted. Combine the good sections with new pieces of scraps to make an interesting rug.

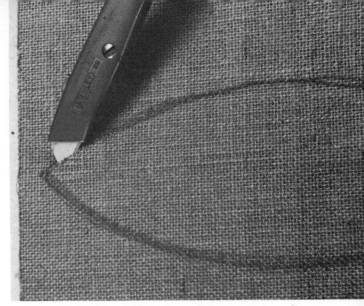

133. To cut rug pieces: Draw your design on burlap backing with crayon, then cut with mat knife from back.

134. "Scroll" detail—draw design on back with crayon, fill in areas with latex paint. Texture of backing comes through painted surface.

135. "Modesto Ash"   30x64"
by Joyce Aiken. Cut green and
white leaf shapes from carpet
pieces and interchange them to
give a positive-negative pattern.

136. "Blueberry Pie I" is
48" in diameter, uses pie-shaped
wedges cut from carpet scraps
arranged in alternating colors.

137. "Blueberry Pie II" has a circle pattern superimposed and cut through pie-shaped wedges, rotated and glued to backing.

138. "Blueberry Pie III" has a second circular pattern cut through wedges. This can be continued as often as you like.

139. "Hexagon" is a crocheted rug that uses
the shell stitch with a heavy wool yarn.

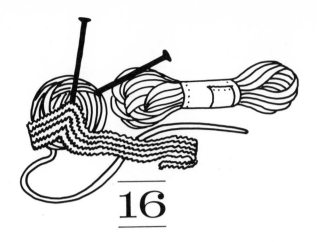

CROCHET AND KNIT RUGS

An easy and effective method of rug making is available to anyone who has already mastered the skills of crocheting and knitting. While many of these rugs are small in size because of difficulty in working on the rug when it gets very large, you can solve this problem by working in sections and sewing the sections together.

The six-sided rug in Plate 139 is crocheted using a clustered shell stitch. Start the rug in the center with a closed chain stitch. Work petal-shaped shells into the center. The next row adds two shells between each of the first six. Each row continues to follow the double shells from the second row with the addition of one extra shell between each of the double shells. Every row adds one more shell to each of the six sides. When the rug is the desired size, add a fringe to finish it.

Plate 140 shows a round, pink and green crocheted rug. It is made of heavy wool yarn, crocheted with a "J" size crochet hook. To make a round rug, put a slip stitch on your crochet hook and chain three stitches. Hook back into the first stitch to close the circle and chain one more stitch to start a new row.

Work around the center with single crochet stitches. When you have completed and closed the circle, chain one stitch and continue around again with a single crochet. To keep the rug flat, add stitches when necessary by crocheting in the same loop twice. Vary some rows by chaining two when you are ready for a new circle, and work double-crochet around the rug in narrow and wide bands.

Change color when you have completed a row and are ready to start a new one. Leave 2 inches of yarn to be pulled through the last stitch in a row when changing color and later work it back into the rug so it does not show. Start the next row with a new color and continue as before. When the last row is finished, choose one of the colors for the fringe.

Drawing 144 shows yarn wrapped around a board about the width of the desired fringe length. Make one cut through the yarn so all the pieces are the same length. A 3-inch fringe needs a piece of yarn about 7 inches long. Plates 141, 142, and 143 show the fringe being added to the rug. Fold the yarn in half and with a crochet hook pull it through a

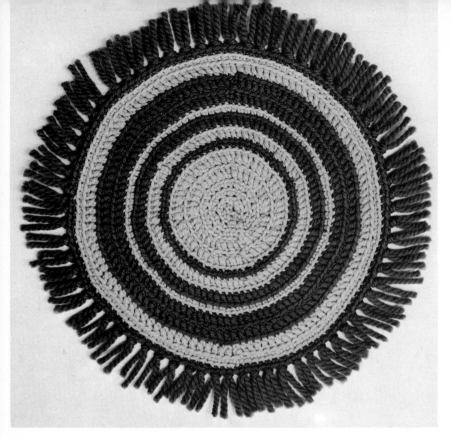

140. "Rings Around the Moon" by Joyce Aiken. Work single and double crochet stitches in bands of pink and lime.

141. Fringe detail—slip a crochet hook through an edge stitch and loop a piece of precut yarn over the hook.

stitch on the edge of the rug. When the yarn loop is large enough, put the two ends through the loop and pull tight. Knot the fringe in every other stitch around the edge.

Detail of another crocheted rug, which also uses the single crochet stitch, appears in Plate 145. Use the largest available crochet hook to crochet torn strips of cotton fabric. This rug, in contrast to the circular rug in Plate 140, is rectangular in shape. To form the rectangle, crochet a chain stitch approximately the width you want for the finished rug. Turn and single crochet across the chain; repeat until the rug is the desired length. Single crochet three rows around the edge to finish.

The rug in Plate 146 is worked in separate bands of crochet, and these bands are then sewn together. Crochet the bands in varying widths—but all the same length. The afghan stitch, shown in detail, is quite different from the single crochet. It looks very much like a woven stitch. When all the bands are finished

they are whipped together on the back. Work an edging of three rows of single crochet around the rug and add a fringe.

Every ecology- or thrift-minded housewife saves plastic bags and bread wrappers. The rug in Plate 147 is made from these bags and wrappers. The plastic does not absorb soil and can easily be hosed off or dipped into a tub of water for cleaning.

Cut the bags into strips about 1 inch wide. Using a large crochet hook, crochet a chain for the center length of the rug. Single crochet around the center line and continue until the rug is the desired size. Add extra stitches on the end curves to keep the rug flat. A detail of the rug in Plate 147 shows stitches of opaque and transparent plastic, some plain and some printed. The colored or printed wrappers can be crocheted in regular bands around the rug to make a pattern.

A collection of the Irish Fisherman, or Aran Isle knitting patterns, are worked into the

2. Gently pull the piece of pre-
t yarn partway through the stitch.

143. Pull the ends of the yarn over
the edge stitch and through the loop.

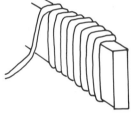

144. For precut fringe,
wrap yarn around a
board, cut along one
edge to make even lengths.

knitted rug in Plate 148. Use a 30″ circular
needle, size 13, to make this rug easier to
handle. The yarn is Orlon acrylic and four
strands are worked at one time. Start the rug
in the center with an Aran Isle border stitch
and use it the entire width of the rug.

Other patterns of the Irish Fisherman,
Plate 149, are used as the knitting progresses
to one end. Pick up stitches at the center
border again, and repeat the pattern to the
other end. This method of working gives you
the mirror image shown in this example. A
border, like the one that runs through the
center of the rug, is knitted in a 4-inch band
around the patterned area. Use macramé
knotting for the fringe on each end.

145. Crochet a rectangular rag rug
from torn strips of cotton fabric using
the largest crochet hook available.

146. "Gold Bars" 20x30" by Joyce Aiken. Crochet bands of color separately, then sew them together. Complete the rug with crocheted edging and fringe. Detail (above) shows strong pattern of afghan stitch made with heavy yarn.

147. Oval rug, crocheted from plastic bags and bread wrappers, uses the single stitch. Detail (opposite) shows pattern interest you get by combining plain and printed wrappers.

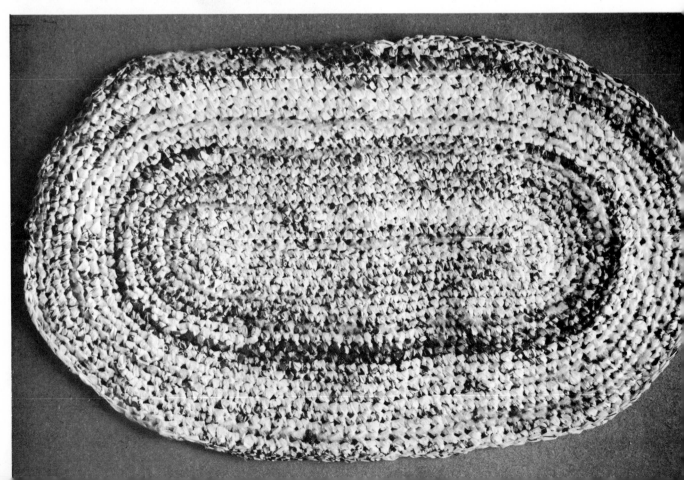

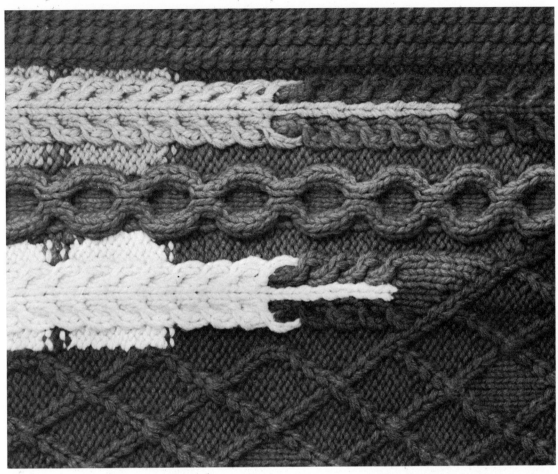

148. "Aran Isle" detail shows the variety of knitted patterns accented by strong colors and value changes.

149. "Aran Isle Variations"   34x71"   by Mark D. Law.
A variety of Irish Fisherman's knitting patterns combine
in this Orlon rug—fringed with macramé knots.

17

BOX AND FRAME RUGS

The box rug is one of the simplest methods of rug making—and one that any child can easily manage. You make a very simple loom from an old wood box, or any other old or new wood frame. Size of the rug is limited by the size of the box, unless a number of these box-sized portions are made and later joined together.

You can make a very simple loom from a fruit crate, Plate 150. Mark off the ends of the crate at ½-inch intervals, and drive a ten-penny nail in at each mark. This means the warp threads are fairly close. Use a heavy cotton string for the warp, stretching from top to bottom of the frame; then weave in strips of cloth from the sides, alternating over and under the cord.

Cut your weaving material into strips about 6 inches longer than the width of the frame. This allows for a 3-inch fringe at each edge. Plate 151 shows fabric strips woven over a cord or string warp, with the extra length shown as they extend at one side to make a fringe.

When the weaving is complete, use a cord to tie a series of slip knots (or half hitches, or any other knot) along the exposed ends of the warp thread to keep the woven strip in place.

Lift the warp threads off the nails for a looped fringe, as in Plate 151; or clip them as in Plate 153.

If you thread the loom with strips of fabric, the ½-inch spacing may not be adequate. If not, wrap the strip around two nails at top, then two at the bottom, instead of wrapping each one. See Plate 153.

Use a long continuous strip of material for weaving, rather than the short strips, to provide a closed edge instead of a fringe, Plate 154.

There are many ways to make frames for this simple weaving. White pine 2x2's make a good frame, with metal reinforcers at the corners, or with C-clamps to hold the boards together. A heavy old picture frame will work, or any heavy wood crate that can be cut down. You can even use an old card table. Cut the inside of the table top away, leaving a frame to which you can tie the warp.

Another rug, woven on a simple box loom, is shown in Plate 155. The warp is double string with rolled fabrics used for the weaving.

For a larger rug, use a folding lawn chair or a metal frame lounger with the canvas cover removed. In either case, tie warp threads the length of the form, with the weaving going crosswise. Stand the frame on end so you will not have to stoop over the furniture to weave.

The rug in Plate 156 is made on a larger frame loom. Tie warp threads (colored grocery store string) onto the loom using three strands, rather than one, for each warp thread. Weave with fabric scraps cut into long strips, to avoid piecing; cut each strip the same length and long enough so that there are 2 inches extra at each end to provide a fringe. Roll the fabric strips to enclose the cut edges. Machine-stitch at each end to hold the weaving in place.

You can buy ready-made simple looms. They are called tapestry frames, hooked rug frames or quilting frames.

The woven rug is a very sturdy one and you can use various kinds of fabrics for the weaving—nylon hose, strips from used clothing, old blankets, draperies and curtains. This method is suited to all ages, and makes no demands upon one's ability to draw.

150. Box frame for weaving rugs starts with a fruit crate.
Nails spaced ½ inch apart along each end hold the string warp.

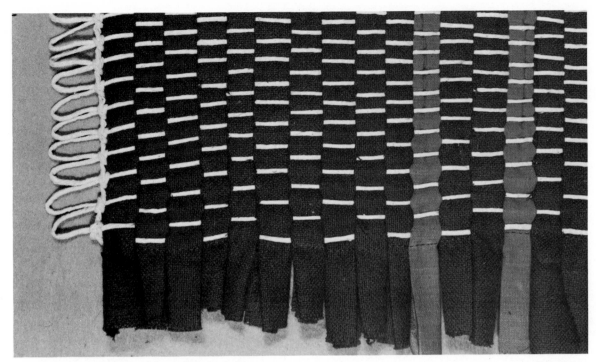

151. Weaving detail—weave fabric strips
through the string warp. Extend extra lengths
of fabric along the sides to form a fringe.

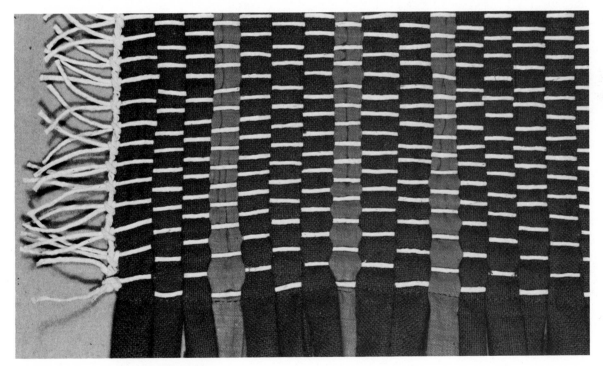

152. Clip string warp threads to make
a fringe at both ends of the rug.

153. When using fabric strips for warp,
wrap them around alternate nails. It is difficult
to weave through them if they are too close.

154. You can use a long continuous strip
of fabric for weaving instead of short strips
to get a closed edge instead of fringe.

155. Rolled fabric strips woven through string
warp make a solid and durable mat or rug. Note the
subtle gradation of colors in both warp and weft.

156. "Confetti" is a 24x36″ rag rug woven on a frame loom.
Warp three strands of string from side to side; weave in rolled
fabric strips of varied thicknesses and colors—lengthwise.

157. "Coffee and Cream"   18x54″   uses nylon
hose, cut and joined into long strips,
then sewn into coils with a blanket stitch.

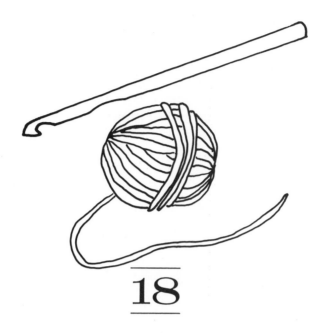

BLANKET STITCH RUGS

Use simple blanket stitch to join coils of cloth, rope, stockings or tubing. Any material you cut into lengths, strips or tubes can be readily made into a rug by this method.

The stitch itself is very simple—even a child can master it with a minimum of instruction. If you are a more practiced seamstress you can control the pattern through the use of regular intervals and even stitches.

Plate 157 shows a blanket stitch rug made from string (or cord) and nylon stockings. Cut the nylons into strips 2 to 3 inches wide and join to make long tubes. (The stockings tend to roll under at the edges, forming tubes as they curl.) By selecting the colors, that is by joining light-colored nylons for some bands, and darker-colored ones in others, you can develop a pattern. Using beiges and browns only, you achieve a rich range of color.

Plate 158 shows the first step of the blanket stitch rug. Tie a knot in the end of the cotton cording (or cotton rope) to prevent raveling and to keep it tight. To make the blanket stitches, thread a large-eyed tapestry or darning needle with yarn, or a heavy thread, cord or string. Draw the yarn around the cotton rope and continue stitching as shown in the photo.

After stitching on the center length, curve the cotton cording so that the cording wraps around itself, remaining flat. The detail in

Plate 159 shows this process. As you wrap the cotton rope around the curved ends, attach two blanket stitches to a single stitch on the preceding coil. This allows for enlarging of the rug and keeps it flat. In attaching one row to the next, insert the needle through the yarn stitch of the preceding row as in Plate 160. Attach the coils by the yarn stitches but do not draw the attaching thread through the rope or tubing. This simplifies the sewing and allows some stretch or "give" to the rug. Rug making with this method is easy and progresses speedily.

Another blanket stitch rug in progress is shown in Plate 161. Make this entirely from men's work pants—denim and twill—by cutting the fabric strips about 3 inches wide with raw edges turned under. Using a double strand of cord (in place of yarn) adds to the durability of the finished piece. If you want the rug to be washable, do not combine wool yarns with cotton strips. Any synthetic yarn or cotton thread or cord will do on cotton fabric.

Cut long plastic bags from the dry cleaners into strips and join, using this blanket stitch method. Other good possibilities are old knitted wool or synthetic sweaters and slips or nightwear. The blanket stitch rug enables you to use almost any discard fabric you have.

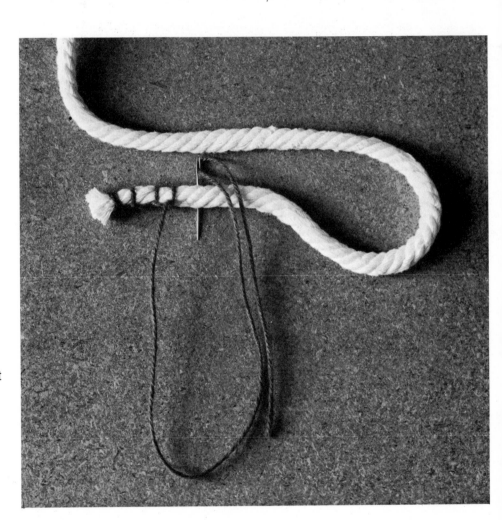

158. To start a cotton rope rug, tie one end with yarn, continue with blanket stitches over rope. Draw up needle into yarn loop to complete the stitch.

159. Attach each coil to preceding one with the blanket stitch. Add extra stitches to allow for the expansions at the curved ends.

160. Each blanket stitch goes over the rope, under the yarn on the preceding row, under the rope and up through the loop. Use a blunt-pointed tapestry needle to pick up the yarn.

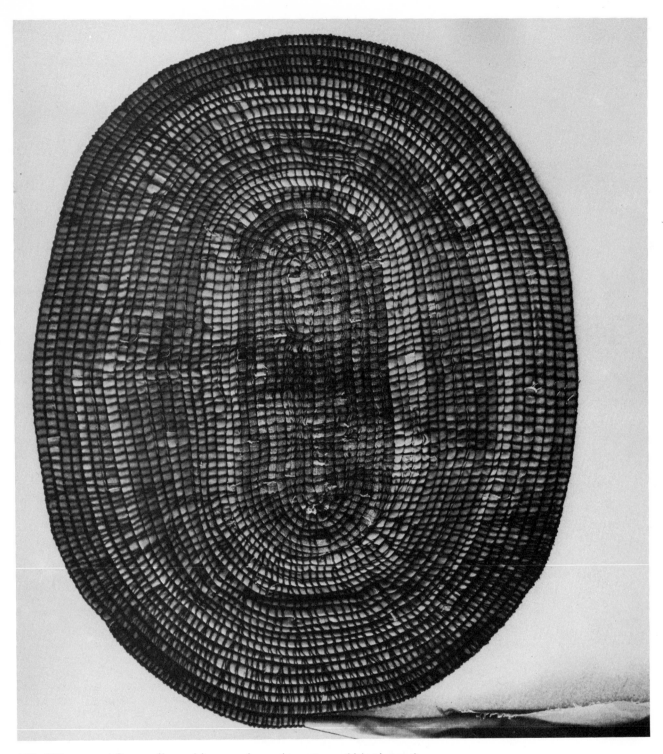

161. "Blues and Greens" combine men's work pants and black cord
to make this durable, sturdy version of the blanket stitch rug.

A Final Word from the Authors

Now that you have some idea of the possibilities, you're ready to plunge into your closet and start making use of the blue jeans, the worn blankets or the out-dated clothes. Making something durable, practical and attractive from discards gives one a sense of accomplishment, and is a gentle bid for ecological good sense.

Once you've experimented and produced rugs for your home, you'll be ready to try a project that will make more demands on your abilities.

When you select or purchase your colors and fabrics, you have greater control over the beauty of the rug. You are also more responsible for it. The sense of accomplishment is great—but seeing the rug in use is even better.

We hope you will have as much fun trying these rug making methods as we have had making our rugs, writing directions and this helpful information. As you work, may laughter warm your heart as your rugs will surely warm your home.

Jean Ray Laury and Joyce Aiken